Race among Friends

The Rutgers Series in Childhood Studies

The Rutgers Series in Childhood Studies is dedicated to increasing our understanding of children and childhoods, past and present, throughout the world. Children's voices and experiences are central. Authors come from a variety of fields, including anthropology, criminal justice, history, literature, psychology, religion, and sociology. The books in this series are intended for students, scholars, practitioners, and those who formulate policies that affect children's everyday lives and futures.

Edited by Myra Bluebond-Langner, Board of Governors Professor of Anthropology, Rutgers University, and True Colours Chair in Palliative Care for Children and Young People, University College London, Institute of Child Health.

ADVISORY BOARD

Perri Klass, New York University
Jill Korbin, Case Western Reserve University
Bambi Schieffelin, New York University
Enid Schildkrout, American Museum of Natural History and Museum for African Art

Race among Friends

. . . .

Exploring Race at a Suburban School

MARIANNE MODICA

Rutgers University Press

New Brunswick, New Jersey and London

Library of Congress Cataloging-in-Publication Data

Modica, Marianne.
    Race among friends : exploring race at a suburban school / Marianne Modica.
        pages cm.—(The Rutgers series in childhood studies) Includes bibliographical refer-
    ences and index.
    ISBN 978-0-8135-7344-1 (hardback)—ISBN 978-0-8135-7343-4 (pbk.)—ISBN
978-0-8135-7345-8 (e-book (epub))
        1. Discrimination in education—United States. 2. Race discrimination—United States.
3. Multicultural education—United States. 4. Post-racialism—United States. 5. Suburban
schools—Social aspects—United States. I. Title.

    LC212.2.M63 2015
    379.2'6—dc23
    2015004944

A British Cataloging-in-Publication record for this book is available from the British Library.

"I, Too" and "Harlem (2)" from *The Collected Poems of Langston Hughes* by Langston Hughes,
edited by Arnold Rampersad with David Roessel, associate editor, copyright © 1994 by the
Estate of Langston Hughes. Used by permission of Alfred A. Knopf, an imprint of the Knopf
Doubleday Publishing Group, a division of Random House LLC. All rights reserved. Additional rights by permission of Harold Ober Associates Incorporated.

Material from this book appeared previously in the journal article "Unpacking the 'Colorblind
Approach': Accusations of Racism at a Friendly, Mixed-Race School," *Race Ethnicity and Education* (December 15, 2014).

Visit our website: http://rutgerspress.rutgers.edu

Manufactured in the United States of America

For my husband, Joseph B. Modica

Contents

Acknowledgments

Like other factors that influence human relations, the way that people think, feel, and act about race is dynamic. The open bigotry and subsequent hostility that once formed the foundation of race relations has, for many, subsided and been replaced by the belief that friendly relations among races are the norm. *Race among Friends* explores tensions that continue to flourish in the midst of those friendly race relations.

Accordingly, I must first thank the students, teachers, and staff at Excellence Academy who allowed me to be a part of their school family. Their honesty and willingness to speak about a sometimes difficult topic paved the way for this work. My special thanks go to students Anthony, Violet, and Lucky, and of course to their teacher, Joann. Her insights during our many hours of conversation were invaluable in helping me to understand all that transpired throughout the hectic days of high school life. My time at Excellence Academy not only resulted in the analysis found in this book but also confirmed something I've known for years: teachers are among the hardest working, most underappreciated people I know.

This project began during my graduate work in the Childhood Studies Department of Rutgers University in Camden, New Jersey. I am so grateful for the leadership of the faculty there, and for their patience with a long-time practitioner who was new to the world of broader theory. Thank you to Drs. Lynne Vallone, Dan Cook, Dan Hart, and Charles Watters. My most special thanks to my advisor, Dr. Lauren Silver, whose guidance and support were crucial and whose friendship I continue to value. My time at

Rutgers was enhanced by the many friendships I formed with my graduate school peers. Thank you Anandini Dar and Patrick Cox, especially, both for your friendship and for pushing me to think of myself as a scholar. The camaraderie we shared made my graduate school experience so much more satisfying. Thanks, also, to Vania Brightman Cox, for your friendship and support.

Over the years I have received much support from administrators, colleagues, and friends at the University of Valley Forge who are too many to name. (You know who you are.) I continue to appreciate their kindness and encouragement. Special thanks to the fabulous librarians who kept me rolling in research through interlibrary loan.

Thanks as well to Peter Mickulas at Rutgers University Press. His belief in the project and his careful, patient, and quick responses smoothed the way of this process.

Finally, all my love to my family and thanks to my husband, Joseph B. Modica (I didn't forget the B), on whose steady support and encouragement I depend for this and every venture.

Race among Friends

Introduction

. . . .

Race, Friendship, and
Multicultural Literature

On a late summer day I sat in a cluttered classroom with Joann Mitchel, a teacher at Excellence Academy (EA).[1] Joann had invited me to participate as a researcher in her tenth and eleventh grade literature classes the following spring. There I would explore the varied and complex ways that students and teachers think about race and act out racial identity as they read multicultural literature (i.e., literature that expressly investigates the experiences of oppressed or marginalized peoples). Since I was familiar with the school, I knew that EA, a suburban charter school, was predominantly white but more racially diverse than its host and neighboring school districts. I asked Joann what I thought was a straightforward question: "What is the racial demographic of your classes?"

Joann looked away, frowned, and then squinted as if trying to remember. Instead of answering my question directly, she told me the following story. A few years ago, while driving home from a conference in the nearby city, Joann got lost for several hours. Finally, as evening loomed, she stopped at a gas station and got out of her car to ask for directions. To Joann's surprise, an elderly black man approached her and said, "Honey, get back in the car." Joann looked at him quizzically. The man nodded toward other African

American males nearby and said, "Don't you see where you are? You're not safe here." Apparently Joann had not noticed that she was the only white person around in a "bad" neighborhood. She took the man's advice and drove away, and after a bit more meandering she finally found the highway that took her back to the safety of the suburbs.

Had Joann told me this story in a different context, I may have thought little of it. Since, however, she was responding to my question about the racial demographic of her students, it seemed clear that Joann's narrative was meant to tell me that she doesn't notice race. Joann was claiming to be colorblind, and she was not alone in her claim. Many saw the 2008 election of our nation's first African American president as an indication that we, as a society, have finally grown past the issue of race. Perhaps, many hoped, a colorblind society was finally within our reach (Choi 2008; Mazzei 2008; Perry 2011).

Colorblind or "Cowards"?

While the election of President Barack Obama was an important milestone in the history of the United States, one need not look very far to see that institutional racism continues in a variety of venues. Prisons are overpopulated with people of color; many neighborhoods remain racially segregated (Anacker 2010; Logan 2011; Seitles 1998); people of color remain disproportionately poor (Hernandez, Denton, and Blanchard 2011; May and Sleeter 2010); and many urban schools, attended primarily by students of color, are underresourced and have far lower test scores and graduation rates than their neighboring whiter suburban school districts (Balfanz and Legters 2004).[2] Perhaps this is why in 2009, less than a year after President Obama's election, Attorney General Eric Holder, who is also African American, stated that we, as Americans, are "a nation of cowards" when it comes to discussing race. Holder insisted, "Though there remain many unresolved racial issues in this nation, we, average Americans, simply do not talk enough with each other about things racial" (qtd. in Thomas and Ryan 2009). The desire to ignore race in favor of a colorblind approach has so permeated America's cultural ethos that many whites, in particular, fear that talking about race in any capacity leaves them open to accusations of racism (Bonilla-Silva 2006; Lewis 2006; Pollock 2004; Tarca 2005).

As a result, race has become a taboo subject in many classrooms, with serious implications for students and teachers. When race is not discussed openly, students are denied the opportunity to think about how race affects them and their relationships with others. Attempts to be colorblind do not end racism; in fact, ignoring race increases the likelihood that racism will occur in schools and in other facets of society (Apfelbaum, Sommers, and Norton 2008; Baldwin 2009; Dixson and Rousseau 2005; Gallagher 2003; Giroux 2008; Haney López 2011; Pollock 2004; Staiger 2005). In light of this, educators face a serious predicament: how can teachers help students to explore issues of race and racism in an environment when talking about race has become increasingly uncomfortable?

Ironically, as Joann was describing her tendency not to notice race, boxes of multicultural literature waiting to be unpacked surrounded us; clearly, Joann believed in the importance of discussing race with her students. Yet, that day as we discussed my project, she found herself in the untenable position of trying to maintain her commitment to social justice while claiming a colorblind approach to race. Through my research I set out to discover how students and teachers construct and perform racial identity as they study multicultural literature in a wider school environment that does not encourage such discussions.

The Element of Friendship

Although Joann was not able to recall the racial backgrounds of her students, she described what she viewed as an important element of her classroom dynamic: the close friendships that existed among the students at the school. She told me at our very first meeting (and reiterated many times after) that her students had known each other for a long time and were very close friends. In keeping with her colorblind stance, Joann did not mention the cross-racial nature of many of these friendships, but once I joined her classes I noticed that aspect of students' friendships almost immediately. Scenes like the following, recorded in my field notes one busy morning, were common:

> I sat at my desk in the corner and watched students mill around, waiting for class to begin. Susan, a white student, picked up the large hand lotion dispenser that sat on Joann's mini refrigerator and carried it to the desk of

Rihanna, an African American student. Susan pumped a blob of lotion out for herself and, without asking permission, squirted some into Rihanna's hand as well. The girls rubbed lotion into their hands for a minute, chatting amicably, until Joann signaled students to get quiet and Susan returned to her seat.

What struck me about this interaction was the familiarity between these eleventh grade girls: their small exchange over the hand lotion was effortless and intimate, and epitomized the nature of the many cross-racial friendships I witnessed at the school. Once I settled in at EA and became involved in class discussions about racism, I realized that friendships such as the one between Rihanna and Susan did not tell the entire story of race relations at the school. As we dug into deeper discussions of multicultural literature, students expressed frustration, anger, and feelings of marginalization over the topic of race. I began to wonder what to make of the strange coexistence of close cross-racial friendships and racial tensions at the school. Therefore, my study developed in an unexpected direction as I looked more closely at these friendships. While students' responses to multicultural literature remained central to my project, I also considered how the context of the school's friendly environment influenced the way students, teachers, and administrators thought and behaved surrounding race. I came to believe that the friendly environment at the school informed ideas and behaviors regarding race for students and teachers alike, complicating race relations for all involved. I found that even in a friendly, suburban environment where students of all racial backgrounds worked and played together harmoniously, race affected the daily experiences of students and teachers in profound but unexamined ways. I argue that rather than create a space for honest and constructive conversations about race, students' cross-racial friendships allowed the space for insensitive responses during class discussions, student silences, and racially biased administrative practices. Consequently, the school's friendly environment did not promote (and may have hindered) deep and productive conversations about race and racial inequity.

Theoretical Foundations

This book is grounded in the work of many scholars who have contributed to understandings of how race informs the lives of youth in and outside of the classroom. My approach and analysis rely on theoretical work in several complementary areas. My work as an emerging scholar in the field of childhood studies informed my approach to this project while critical race theory and models of racial identity development were useful in my analysis. Additionally, the important works of numerous ethnographers who studied the impact of race in educational contexts helped me to understand the complex behaviors and interactions I witnessed and participated in at Excellence Academy.

Critical Race Theory

At the foundation of my work is the premise that race continues to be a crucial factor in maintaining the hierarchical power structures upon which our society was built; I believe that racism is a present and prevalent social problem. Because of my focus on exploring the effects of racism in education, I use critical race theory (CRT) as the organizing scheme of this book. CRT originated in legal scholarship and examines the intersection of race and power and, over the last several decades, has become a methodological tool to analyze and critique structures of inequity in education (Ladson-Billings and Tate 1995; Solorzano and Yosso 2009). Several key concepts of CRT were foundational in my analysis.

First, while recognizing the intersection of race with factors such as social class and gender in explaining societal inequity (Kumasi 2011), CRT insists that racism is a contemporary and persistent force that shapes the lives of every citizen on macro and micro levels (Cerezo et al. 2013; Perry 2011), and that it is typical of the American experience (Delgado and Stefancic 2000). Gloria Ladson-Billings and William F. Tate (1995) stress the need to consider how race influences educational quality and experiences, stating, "class- and gender-based explanations are not powerful enough to explain all of the difference (or variance) in school experience and performance" (51). Because racial inequity persists, the concept of societal transformation is an implicit and crucial objective of CRT (DeCuir and Dixson 2004). Infused with the goal of social justice, this area of study privileges the voices of traditionally oppressed groups and insists that societal progress toward racial equality in part depends on whites, as members of the powerful dominant culture, becoming aware of racism and incorporating a racial identity that moves them toward antiracist action.

One explanation for the persistence of race as a significant factor in power relations is the notion, derived from critical legal studies, that whiteness functions as a valuable form of property, granting rights of citizenship to those who possess it that others cannot claim (Harris 1993). According to Imani Perry (2011), whiteness as property functions on several levels simultaneously: wealth, income, worth of possessions, financial power, and the likelihood of future financial success are all influenced by race. Additional examples of the benefits of whiteness are many. At EA and in many educational settings, the cultural practices of whites are valued above others and form the language and behavioral norm against which all others are evaluated (Baldwin 2009; Law 1999); in this sense, whiteness serves as an access-granting commodity for students. The manner in which educational funding is derived from real estate taxes is a tangible way that whiteness works as property, since past and present racist housing policies ensure that whites are most likely to own more highly valued real estate (Logan 2011; Seitles 1998). Derrick Bell (2000), one of the founders of CRT, notes that even whites who are not affluent gain something from their whiteness: the feeling of racial superiority (DiAngelo 2006). Peggy McIntosh (2005) expands on the concept of whiteness as property in her seminal essay on white privilege. She uses the metaphor of an "invisible knapsack" to describe the way in which whites benefit from, but fail to recognize, their privileged status. According to McIntosh, contained in that metaphorical backpack are the many unearned benefits that work to keep whites in a position of societal dominance.

A second key concept of CRT is Bell's theory of interest convergence. Bell (1992) argues that many whites will pursue racial justice only when it is in their best interests to do so. Conversely, when whites perceive that adherence to nondiscriminatory policies will result in some form of loss, they will cease to subscribe to racially just belief or conduct. Although whites may "agree in the abstract" that African Americans "are entitled to constitutional protection against racial discrimination" (Bell 2009, 75), rarely would they agree to practices that might decrease their economic and societal dominance. When legal actions result in policies that threaten to displace whites from their historical position of power, whites will often employ discourses to weaken the effect of such policies.

One particularly ubiquitous discourse, cited by Bell (2009) as a prime example of interest convergence among whites, is that of "reverse racism," often taking the form of anti–affirmative action arguments. Through this discourse many whites assert that they are the new victims of discrimination and are suffering because of the unmerited advancement of people of color. The aspiration toward race neutrality or colorblindness inherent in reverse racism discourse allows whites to retain both their privileged status and the façade of egalitarian belief (Baldwin 2009); thus, through claims that considering race in any way is unfair, whites preserve the appearance of fairness while maintaining the social dominance that is in their best interests. Examples of whites engaging reverse racism and related discourses are well documented. Eduardo Bonilla-Silva (2006) describes how white college students used Freudian projection in the form of reverse racism arguments, either claiming that people of color "are the racist ones" (63) or that affirmative action initiatives make blacks feel "kind of inferior" (65). Other white students believed that they had no ethnicity or culture, and envied those whose ethnicity allowed them to apply for college scholarships (Perry 2002). Some whites espoused stereotypes about the "laziness" of African Americans, comparing them to supposedly more industrious whites who lose out on opportunity due to reverse racism (Trainor 2008).

Other closely related discourses that whites employed to deny their position of dominance involve claiming they were unjustly blamed for racial inequity (Kromidas 2012; Lewis 2006) and denying the salience of race by using class or culture as explanations of inequality (Bucholtz 2011). Some whites expressed envy and resentment at the group cohesiveness that they imagined people of color experience (Marx 2006) and cast themselves as direct victims of racism by blacks (McIntyre 1997) or as victims of other types of discriminatory behavior, such as "blonde jokes" (Haviland 2008). Whites also embraced "exception to the rule stories" about famous African Americans to argue against the existence of structural racism (McIntyre 1997; Perry 2011)—the election of President Obama supports that particular narrative nicely. Adherence to these discourses allows whites to retain racial dominance (i.e., to preserve their racial interests) while avoiding the appearance of racism since such arguments are often used to demand fairness and equality. Reverse racism and accompanying narratives are so highly proliferated among whites that it not surprising to hear white youth echo these larger societal beliefs (Bucholtz 2011); after teaching college students for many years, I am more surprised when some variation of this discourse is *not* expressed during class discussions of race.

While the reverse racism discourse is often used to emphasize the importance of fairness in a colorblind meritocracy, as Bell (2009) pointed out, whites may not act on this belief when they feel their position of dominance is threatened. Frank L. Samson (2013) found that white college students recommended changing college admission standards when faced with a scenario that depicted Asian Americans, and not whites, as the majority of incoming freshman. In that circumstance, white students altered the weight given to class rankings and test score percentiles in order to ensure that whites would remain the majority of the admitted student group.

The importance of storytelling and counternarrative is a third central idea of CRT. Through counternarrative, people of color tell and retell their own stories, using the understandings they have gained through experience to succeed in all areas of life (Cerezo et al. 2013). By valuing the varied experiential knowledge and giving voice to people who have been racially oppressed (Dixson and Rousseau 2005; Kumasi 2011; Ladson-Billings and Tate 1995), counternarrative exposes and challenges the racist narratives whites have historically used to normalize white dominance. CRT utilizes three forms of counterstorytelling: individuals' personal narratives, experiences with oppression told in the third person voice, and combined counternarratives that compile data to "create composite characters and place them in social, historical, and political situations" (Solorzano and Yosso 2009, 139).

Hearing the Voices of Youth

Because of its emphasis on social policy and children's rights (Bass 2010), the theoretical framework of childhood studies compliments CRT's focus on giving voice to historically marginalized people. Rather than viewing childhood as a means to achieving a future goal (i.e., the maturity of adulthood), childhood studies scholars emphasize the need to respect the voices and rights of children in the present (Tisdall and Punch 2012). With early roots in sociology, this interdisciplinary field views childhood as a socially constructed status (Jenks 1996) that varies throughout time and place. Therefore, by studying the experiences of past and present children in a variety of settings and through examining depictions of childhood in art, literature, film, and other media, childhood studies scholars challenge and deconstruct societal tropes about childhood. Allison James

(2007) explains that at the core of childhood studies "is a conception of children as articulate social actors who have much to say about the world" (261). She argues that it is not enough to allow children opportunity to express their opinions; researchers must heed children's viewpoints to understand the complexities of our social world. Debra Van Ausdale and Joe R. Feagin (2001) warn against "adultcentric" interpretations of children's experiences, wherein "adults interpret children's activities in comparison to adult conceptions of what children *should* be doing, rather than what they are *actually* doing" (3). Thus, throughout this book I give priority to the thoughts, ideas, and opinions that students voiced as they studied multicultural literature, in the hopes that those voices will help us to understand how race continues to function in educational settings.

Exploring Race through Literature

I began this work convinced that literature is a powerful and important tool in helping students shape understandings and construct identities as they internalize dominant cultural meanings (Botelho and Rudman 2009; Brooks 2008; Trainor 2008). Multicultural literature, in particular, may help students think about issues of social justice that they may not be aware of in their everyday lives. However, for some students, merely reading multicultural literature will not necessarily lead to antiracist understandings. Instead, students may express racially intolerant attitudes as they interpret these texts. For example, while reading Maya Angelou's *I Know Why the Caged Bird Sings* (1969), white high school students alternately praised Angelou for being an exception to the rule (i.e., an African American who "made it") and accused her of being a racist who was intolerant of whites and who blamed whites for her problems (Trainor 2008). Similarly, white college students in a teacher education program worried that white children reading Mildred Taylor's award-winning *Roll of Thunder, Hear My Cry* (1976) would "feel bad" about the negative portrayal of whites in the novel (Saul and Wallace 2002). Other studies had more mixed results: one group of white preservice teachers insisted that Lynne Reid Banks's *The Indian in the Cupboard* (1980) should be included in the curriculum because it is an "engaging" story and because there were no Native American children in the classes these preservice teachers served. This group did not consider the effect of racist stereotypes in children's books on the white students who read them. However, after continued discussion some students came to admit the inherent racism and possibly damaging effect of the story (Cochran-Smith 2004). Beverley Naidoo (1992) also experienced mixed results in her study of how white, British high school students responded to multicultural fiction. While many students responded positively to the literature, some remained defensive and resisted ideas of white hegemony.

Further, teachers' understandings of race are an integral part of how class discussions surrounding multicultural texts unfold. Naidoo (1992) notes that the English teacher in her study failed to reflect on his own racist assumptions and so was ill equipped to help students do the uncomfortable work of recognizing racial privilege in their everyday lives. White teachers who have not reflected on their own position of racial dominance may inadvertently transmit their narrow views on race to their students through the same whiteness discourses that are incorporated into their racial identity, thereby reproducing in their students the feelings and beliefs that perpetuate racist structures (McIntyre 1997; Sleeter 2005). Even teachers who mean to expose racism may find it difficult to break this cycle: one white teacher, for example, who added multicultural literature to her curriculum after being called a racist by an African American student continued to use language and practices that placed whiteness as the norm and discouraged students from thinking about racial power and privilege in contemporary society (Hollingworth 2009).

These studies have shown that reading literature meant to produce deeper understandings of societal inequity and foster attitudes of tolerance may instead provide an outlet for the intolerant attitudes students and teachers hold. At EA, discussions of multicultural literature revealed the potent and unresolved feelings that students harbored surrounding the subject of racism and provided the means for students, teachers, and administrators to express a wide gamut of ideas about race that sometimes stood in contrast to the school's outwardly friendly environment.

Race among Friends

While many scholars have examined race relations among students in conflict-ridden school environments, racially diverse schools with harmonious student and staff relations remain understudied spaces. What is more, while some studies have analyzed the prevalence and quality of cross-racial friendships in schools, the effect of these friendships on students' racial identities and on student–staff relations is especially underexamined.

Several researchers have explored the effect of attending school in a multiracial environment on students' inclination to form cross-race friendships, and some have compared the quality of same-race and cross-race friendships at those schools. Since racial integration provides students with the opportunity to meet peers of varying backgrounds, it is not surprising that students in racially diverse schools are more likely to have cross-race friends than those in homogenous settings. More significantly, white students in racially diverse schools were less likely to explain racial exclusion through the use of racial stereotypes and were more likely to say that exclusion based on race is wrong (Killen et al. 2010). However, other studies show that although the likelihood of cross-race friendships increased in racially diverse settings, students continued to prefer same-race friendships (Munniksma and Juvonen 2012; Tavares 2011), and the quality of same and cross-race friendships differed in some aspects. For example, while same and cross-race friends reported equal levels of loyalty and emotional security within their relationships, students reported lower intimacy rates with their cross-race friends (Aboud, Mendelson, and Purdy 2003), perhaps because, as data from the National Longitudinal Study of Adolescent Health showed, cross-racial friends were less likely to spend time together in shared activities (Kao and Joyner 2004). Adolescents' proclivity to form intense "best friendships" is well known, but these self-proclaimed best friendships were less likely to occur cross-racially, and when they did occur they were less stable over time (Rude and Herda 2010). In spite of these limitations, studies support the idea that a racially diverse setting is important to encourage cross-racial friendships among youth (Munniksma and Juvonen 2012; Quillian and Campbell 2003; Tavares 2011).

Cross-racial friendships influence students' behaviors in more specific ways as well. In some cases, students used humor within and surrounding their friendships to work through their racial positioning and navigate the role of race in their lives. Elementary school children in a mixed-race, mixed-class area of New York City used racial joking within their friendship groups to traverse racial boundaries, that is, to appropriate language and cultural styles they might not otherwise have access to (Kromidas 2012). Despite the concerns of the adults around them, British high school students in a mixed-race setting told racist jokes within cross-race friendship groups and claimed that this practice proved they were not racist (Pettigrew 2011).

Friendships across race also influenced the demeanor that African American students presented to whites at school. Apprehensive that their white peers and teachers would unfairly ascribe stereotypical behavior (such as fighting) to them, African American males attending a white-dominated school for several years were concerned with behaving in ways that countered the racialized typecast of the unruly, disruptive black male. For these students, "there was a clear and constant struggle . . . to combat the racist stereotypes in an effort to negate the self-fulfilling prophecy" (Matrenec 2011, 238).

These studies show that, as I found at EA, students and teachers can embody race through cross-racial relationships in complex ways. While children and youth undoubtedly benefit from friendships with diverse groups of peers, educators cannot assume that convivial relations indicate a "post-racial" status and make thinking and talking about race unnecessary.

Studying Racial Identity

Inspired by CRT, the qualitative investigations I have mentioned are rooted in the desire to move toward a more racially just society. Theories of racial identity development share a similar goal and added a helpful dimension to my understanding of the perspectives of youth and adults at EA. Throughout this work I use the term *racial identity* broadly. For my purposes, participants' ascription of selves and others as members of particular, socially constructed, hierarchical racial groups; their identifications with racially based cultural cliques; and the opinions they shared about race were all indications of racial identity. Scholarship on racial identity helped me determine what specific attitudes and behaviors regarding race were most important for the focus of this work.

Janet Helms (1990) describes racial identity as a developmental process wherein people are positioned along a continuum of statuses or profiles of racial awareness and beliefs (Carter, Helms, and Juby 2004).[3] This psychological perspective attempts to understand people's behavioral dispositions by analyzing their location along the racial identity continuum (Abrams and Trusty 2004; Hays, Chang, and Havice 2008; Helms 2007; Silvestri and Richardson 2001). Psychological models of racial identity formation do not suggest that all individuals pass through levels of racial identity in a strict hierarchy (Quintana 2007; Tatum 1997; Worrell, Cross, and Vandiver 2001) but claim that developmental commonalities exist for people who grow up in places where whiteness is privileged, regardless of their racial backgrounds. In the United States, all students internalize whiteness as the standard of normalcy at a young age because they are influenced by cultural images that reinforce stereotypes and elevate whiteness as the standard of beauty (Winkler 2012). In addition, developmental racial identity theories view alignment with antiracist belief as the end goal of racial self-actualization for individuals of all racial backgrounds (Helms 1990; Tatum 1997).

Aside from these commonalities, racial identity models suggest that the journey toward racial actualization follows divergent paths for people of color and for whites. For people of color, awareness of the existence of racial inequity usually comes later in childhood or during adolescence through exposure to racism in some form (Quintana 2007). As they move along the continuum of racial identity profiles, self-actualized racial identity may require students of color to immerse themselves in their own cultural backgrounds to the exclusion of others for a time so that they can dispel internalized standards of white superiority, come to value their own heritage, and become committed to social activism (Helms 1990). Both a feeling of connectedness with their racial group and a critical awareness of racism are necessary components of positive racial identity development in youth of color (Quintana 2007).

Whites, immersed in dominant cultural values, may think little about race unless racism becomes visible through relationships with people of color or by some other means (such as media exposure to racism). Whites may then experience guilt, shame, or anger, and respond by either avoiding people of color or developing discourses that absolve themselves from responsibility for racism. If they do not move beyond these negative feelings, whites may stagnate in beliefs that disallow them from facing the reality of present-day racism, and may employ one or more discourses to avoid recognizing their own position of power in a white-dominated culture. Those who progress toward a self-actualized racial identity find ways to grow past guilt and anger and become advocates of racial justice. For whites, fully actualized racial identity formation culminates in the assuming of an antiracist persona (Helms 1990; Tatum 1997).

One might reasonably ask, is racial identity for whites only about progressing through a developmental continuum that leads to antiracism? Don't whites also need to experience pride in their racial heritage? David R. Roediger (1994) reminds us that race is and always has been about power.

Racial categories are socially constructed and were intentionally developed by whites in order to create and maintain a strict power hierarchy, with whites firmly positioned at the top. Historically, the purpose of whiteness as a racial category has been to advantage whites by denying rights and opportunity to people of color. Without this purpose, there would be no need for whiteness or any other racial category (Fine 1997). Therefore, while racial self-actualization for people of color involves finding that which was denied to them through centuries of subordination—that is, pride in their racial heritage and a sense of belonging as fully equal members of society— for whites, the road to a fully realized racial identity involves recognizing the privilege gained through centuries of domination and finding ways to work toward undoing the negative societal effects that remain as the product of racism.

This working toward racial justice is the definition of *antiracism*. I lean heavily on Beverly Daniel Tatum's (1997) explanation of antiracism in my thinking and, on one occasion, shared her ideas on the topic with an eleventh grade class (with surprising results; see chapter 4). Tatum describes three possible ways of behaving regarding racism: active racism, passive racism, and antiracism. People engaged in active racism behave in blatantly racist ways while passive racists may not initiate racist behavior but may collude with such behavior through silence. Those who are antiracist actively work to combat racism through their words and deeds.

I do not subscribe to the idea that a complex construct like racial identity can be essentialized into neatly packaged developmental stages, nor do I try to determine the specific racial identity status of individual youth or adults. However, keeping in mind the psychological approach to racial identity development helped me in two ways throughout this project. First, this developmental approach defines antiracism as the culmination of racial self-actualization and, therefore, reminds us to avoid a form of uncritical multiculturalism wherein we "celebrate difference" but fail to explore realities of class struggle, poverty, and disenfranchisement experienced by groups outside of the white, middle-class experience (McCarthy and Dimitriadis 2005). Second, since these theories view individual's subscription to racialized discourses as indicative of their identity status, psychological theories of racial identity helped me to analyze the arguments that students used as an indication of their position regarding denial or acceptance of antiracist ideals.

Methods

Excellence Academy is a public charter school located in Woodlark, a predominantly white suburban town of approximately 32,000, located thirty miles from a large northeastern city. The school website describes EA as 60 percent white, 20 percent African American, 9 percent multiracial, 5 percent Asian / Pacific Islander, and 5 percent Hispanic. Since 26 percent of students at EA receive free or reduced rate lunch, the school is both more racially and economically diverse than its neighboring districts.[4] EA draws 36 percent of its students from the Carltonville Area School District, a larger and more diverse district located twelve miles away. Many students in Joann's classes live in Carltonville and travel over an hour each way by school bus to attend EA.

Out of Joann's ninety-five literature students, only five were Asian. These were of Indian and Chinese background, and, fulfilling the "model minority" stereotype (Shankar 2008; Song 2001; Wong et al. 1998), all were in honors classes and tended toward close friendships with white students. There was only one Latina in Joann's classes, who sat mostly with African American students both in homeroom and in class. Hence, my analysis tends to focus on interactions between African American and white students. In keeping with the white/black dichotomy prevalent in U.S. race relations (Winkler 2012), it was between these groups that racial boundaries and tensions seemed most prevalent.

Like most other high schools in the United States, EA's classes were academically tracked; therefore, Joann taught an "honors" and "on level" version of her tenth and eleventh grade literature classes. The school used the term "on level" euphemistically for classes that were composed of any students who were not in the honors group, regardless of their actual academic performance. The relationship between academic tracking and race is a longstanding, controversial, and complicated subject. Although this work adopts a broader focus, the de facto racial segregation caused by academic tracking at EA was intricately connected with teacher expectations, pedagogy, classroom management decisions, and students' perceptions: all of these worked together to influence racial identity in ways too important to ignore. This book addresses the way that academic tracking created boundaries among students and influenced student and teacher perceptions, educational opportunities, and cross-racial friendships at EA.

Participant Observation

For five months I arrived at Joann's homeroom at 8 A.M. and remained with her, sometimes as a quiet observer and sometimes as an active participant, through homeroom, four literature classes, lunch, a prep period, and a "flex" study period that rotated daily through several different groups of students. In exchange for being allowed to participate in Joann's classes, I offered myself to work with individual students or small groups who might need some extra help. In this way I adopted the role of participant observer that is common to ethnographers. I took field notes, wrote memos, and conducted interviews with students, teachers, and administrators. The interview segments I include provide the voice of the youth in this study; my dependence on CRT and childhood studies as theoretical frameworks led me to center my analysis around these voices, and I found that many students were eager to tell their stories. Some African American students, especially, were so enthusiastic about sharing their experiences that more than a year after I had completed my field work they voluntarily created a map of their neighborhood for me, detailing the racial demographics of the area and their perception of criminal activity of specific blocks, playgrounds, and parking lots.

I was fortunate that Joann was an open and enthusiastic research partner, willing to do the difficult labor of exploring not only her students' racial identities but her own identity as a white person as well. Through our many conversations over the five months we spent together, Joann often expressed her concern about racial inequity and her desire to help educate her students in issues of social justice. Yet Joann admitted to me many times that she felt unsure and uncomfortable in her attempts to add race to her curriculum. Joann's willingness to explore her own feelings about race deepened my study considerably, enabling me to analyze the discomfort that white teachers often experience over the topic of race.

Anthropologists have noted the awkward space of participant observation; researchers must form relationships with the people they are studying while maintaining the distance that thoughtful analysis requires (Hume and Mulcock 2004). When I began my research at EA, I did not worry about maintaining appropriate distance from the students since I knew they would view me as an outsider. I worried more about my ability to establish an open, friendly rapport with students so they would feel comfortable with me and be willing to share their ideas freely. While a younger ethnographer, like Mary Bucholtz (2011), might hope to blend in and avoid alignment with teachers, I recognized from the start that my age, demeanor, and status as an adult helper would likely cause students to view me as an authority figure. The fact that Joann introduced me to students as a college professor (as in, "Isn't it great, we have a college professor to help us in our class!") and that she would occasionally leave me "in charge" while she used the bathroom or ran a quick errand compromised my attempts to maintain a low profile.

Nancy Mandell (1988) advocates that researchers of children adopt the "least-adult role," through which the researcher puts aside adult "authority, verbal competency, cognitive, and social mastery" (438) while interacting with young subjects. Although I knew that the students at EA would view me as an authority figure no matter what I did, I tried to distance myself from the role of teacher as much as possible. For instance, in order to leave class for any reason, students were required to have agenda books signed by teachers, with time and date noted. Students often approached me to sign their agendas, but I consistently refused, explaining that I was not a teacher and did not have the authority to grant the permission they sought. Additionally, I was careful to remain uninvolved in any disciplinary matters, never correcting behavior no matter how obviously students broke school rules. The students quickly realized that I could be relied on to keep a secret and might even function as a co-conspirator in their harmless breaking of rules. For example, students who were denied permission to leave the room would often surreptitiously ask me to get them a water bottle or snack from the vending machine in the hallway, which I would do, sometimes providing the change they needed to complete the purchase.

My Racial Identity

Like all white people who grow up in the United States, I have experienced the privilege of being part of the dominant racial group over the course of my life. Therefore, I knew that I would need to reflect on my own racial identity throughout this project, continually monitoring my own feelings about the students and teachers at EA, especially as discussions about race developed. I hoped that my years of talking about race with college students who were not very much older would help me to relate to these high school students. However, I also knew that I needed to maintain a continual awareness of how my whiteness would affect my relationships with students and teachers at EA.

Beginning a new position in any context can be awkward, and my first few weeks at EA certainly contained awkward moments. Sometimes I didn't quite know what to do with myself. Should I sit quietly at my little desk in the corner of the room or float around near students' tables as they worked together in groups? Should I initiate conversations with students or wait for them to get desperate enough with an assignment to turn to me for assistance? I used both of these approaches, and students were accustomed enough to having random adults in the room to either ignore me or make eye contact if they needed help. The one task that caused me to create a field note category titled "Feeling Like a Stupid White Person" was my attempt to learn students' names. Joann had provided me with a student list for each class, which I studied diligently from day one. Yet I had trouble remembering and pronouncing some of the students' names, and I noticed that it was not the Anglo names with which I struggled. Names like "Sue" or "John" stuck like glue on the first pass. However, the "ethnic" names—and even my use of that term shows my own intractable ethnocentricity—were difficult for me to hear clearly and remember. At times I would ask students to repeat their names so that I could be sure I was hearing and learning them correctly. During this process there were a few times that, to spare us both the embarrassment, I made believe I had mastered the student's name and then ran to Joann for help when class was over. I recognize that part of my struggle to remember these names involved lack of familiarity; I know that our brains learn by relating new information to that which we already know. Still, I worried that by stumbling over students' "ethnic"-sounding names I would create the impression among students that I thought these names were exotic or strange. I did not want the students of color to view me as insensitive, nor did I want to embarrass them by mispronouncing their names. Of course, within a week or so I did learn all the students' names, and this mini-crisis passed. I relate it here as an example of the anxiety about race that is an element of my own white racial identity.

No research is value neutral (Mills and Gale 2007), and I came to this project with many beliefs that are part of my racial identity. I believe that racism is a very real and present problem on individual and structural levels and that it is the responsibility of every citizen to work toward a just society. What is more, through racist actions whites originated the problem of racial inequity and, therefore, we must do all we can to work against present-day forms of racism (Katz 1978; Lewis 2006). As a researcher, I recognized the danger in coming into a project such as this with such strong opinions; I might be the opposite of colorblind and harbor a hypersensitivity that would see racism everywhere. Added to this is the fact that I had a professional interest in finding racist discourse at my site in order to validate the need for my research. While we cannot ignore our personal biases, it is essential that ethnographers diligently pursue the perspectives of all research participants and not privilege the experiences of some participants over others (Forsey 2004). For me, this meant I must try to understand the perspectives of white students and teachers whose ideas about racism were different from my own. Jennifer Seibel Trainor (2008) warns of the danger of analysis that ends with the "gotcha!" moment (15), and I knew that I needed to avoid the self-satisfying practice of justifying my own preconceptions by focusing on the racism of other whites. Instead, my goal was to pursue, as Bucholtz (2011) describes, the "co-construction of cultural meaning" that is inherent in ethnographic research, wherein data is "jointly produced in the encounter between researcher and researched and then recontextualized through analysis and writing" (37).

Taking the Time to Listen

When I began my fieldwork at EA, my intention was to study the influence of multicultural literature on students' construction of racial identity, and I imagined most of my analysis would involve students' direct responses to those texts. I found that although students did respond to the texts in important ways, my study was greatly enriched by my daily observations and interactions with students throughout the entire school day. Through the hours of intense discussion, mind-numbing tedium, cheerful conviviality, and, on occasion, high drama that make up the high school experience, the themes of this work emerged. I did not embark on this project with the intention of studying cross-racial friendships; that theme materialized as I listened to students and teachers and observed their interactions over the course of the months that I spent at the school. As Ruth Emond (2009) points out, "ethnography takes time" (137). It is my hope that my time at EA was well spent and that the resulting work will advance our understanding of the complicated and ever-changing processes that inform racial identity development in youth.

Chapter Overview

Chapter 1 examines how students performed race amid their cross-racial friendships and how, in spite of these friendships, racial identity for students and teachers was imbued with the struggle for power. I describe how students performed race through physical appearance, speech, participation in identity groups such as "jocks" and "nerds," and other behaviors. Students maintained racial boundaries, sometimes permeable but often fixed, through categorizing behaviors as "acting white" or "acting black," and were quick to correct errant friends who might cross these performance boundaries. While African American students denied that racial performance was connected to academic achievement, they also acknowledged their underrepresentation in the school's honors classes. Teachers and administrators maintained an academic hierarchy related to race through academic placement of students and through curricular choices. This chapter will show that, in the midst of an overall friendly environment, students were both producers and products of a defined racial geography that perpetuated power structures among them.

Chapter 2 looks more closely at the racial tensions that existed beneath the surface of this friendly school environment. Even while "we all get along here" was the prevailing mantra, students and teachers felt marginalized over the issue of race for a variety of reasons. African American students felt that their background was ignored while white students and teachers feared accusations of racism or felt they were the victims of reverse racism. As the result of these usually unspoken tensions, a tenth grade discussion of Ishmael Beah's *A Long Way Gone* (2007) erupted into an argument that left Joann and her students upset and with no resolution of their feelings of marginalization. Instead, racial tensions were pushed safely back beneath the surface while, outwardly, students continued to "get along" with one another.

Chapters 3 and 4 explore the responses of the eleventh grade honors class to the poetry of Langston Hughes and *The Bluest Eye* by Toni Morrison (1970). This class stood out both for the complexity of students' responses to the texts and for the consistent claims of close cross-racial friendships among them. These chapters examine how students' friendships informed responses to this multicultural literature. During study of the Hughes's poetry, students created contextualized discourses to resist talking about racism and deny its salience in their present reality. Throughout both these units of study, a group of vocal white students dominated class discussions and did not incorporate their African American friends' perspectives into their increasingly angry responses. Lighter-skinned African American students tended to side with whites during class discussions, leading me to consider the effects of colorism (in-group discrimination based on skin tone) on the students in this class. The angry responses of white students reached a crescendo on the last two days of *The Bluest Eye* unit. At the same time African American students grew steadily more silent on the topic. I analyze the anger, resistance, and silence students displayed within the context of students' friendships to discover what these varied responses reveal about students' racial identities.

The concluding chapter argues that schools should consider the continuing influence of race on their policies and practices, even in friendly educational settings like the one highlighted in this work. I recommend ways that schools can facilitate broader understandings among students of how race continues to affect their lives and the lives of their friends. Then, as I examine more deeply the complicated influence of cross-racial proximity and friendship on students' racial identities, I explore the emotional place that students spoke from in their angry responses regarding race and the possible reasons for the silence of other white and African American students in the face of this anger. Finally, I suggest ways to encourage and support students and teachers' participation in continued classroom conversations about race.

1

Boundaries among Friends

■ ■ ■ ■ ■ ■ ■ ■ ■ ■ ■ ■ ■ ■ ■ ■

Performing Race and Policing Its Boundaries

One thing the folks at Excellence Academy agreed on was that the school was a friendly place. Students of various races, ethnicities, and grade levels, guys and girls together, milled about freely, chatting and laughing behind the stacks of books they carried from class to class. Research on cross-racial friendships among students has shown that when students of differing racial backgrounds attend school together, "school propinquity effect" (Quillian and Campbell 2003, 561) takes hold; that is, because of their proximity to one another, students in more diverse schools are more likely to form cross-racial friendships (Killen et al. 2010; Munniksma and Juvonen 2012; Rude and Herda 2010; Tavares 2011). This seemed to be the case at EA. Had I spent only a week or two there, I might have come away with the belief that students, teachers, and administrators had reached some kind of racial nirvana; the school seemed to serve as a model of racial harmony. There was no doubt that friendships flourished and that the school provided a safe, comfortable learning environment.

In all of Joann's classes I noticed friendships that crossed racial boundaries. Sometimes students' friendships were obvious, as students sat together in class or ate lunch together every day, but at other times I was surprised by a hug, a backrub, a high five, or even a half-joking "I love you" between students of different racial backgrounds that I had not known were friends. Joann had mentioned before I began my fieldwork that many of the students had "been together since kindergarten" and remained close friends, a fact that students confirmed during interviews. However, by the students' own accounts, interracial friendships between white and African American students existed within the context of behavioral boundaries. Students accepted these cross-racial friendships as long as one continued to "act" as a member of one's own race. Those who crossed these performance boundaries risked the disapproval of their peers (Bucholtz 2011; Tyson 2011), and students often discussed their views regarding what was and was not expected and acceptable behavior according to racial ascription.

If, as Van Ausdale and Feagin (2001) have shown, children as young as four years old act out the deep-seated racialized identity roles that surround them, we would expect high school students to do the same. This chapter explores the ways that students at EA performed race daily within socially constructed language and behavioral boundaries. In the midst of the cross-racial friendships that existed at the school, students ascribed racial categories to one another and constructed borders around those categories, "set up to define the places that are safe and unsafe, to distinguish *us* from *them*" (Anzaldúa 1999, 25). Racial boundaries at EA were sometimes firm and other times porous, and often policed by students. Since the power dynamics that have infused race relations for generations continue in educational settings (Bucholtz 2011; Chalmers 1997; Lewis 2006), it is not surprising that, at EA, racial identity for students and teachers was imbued with the quest to gain and maintain power. I will describe how students expressed racial identity through language, physical appearance, religiosity, use of physical space, and ascription of identity groupings, and how they maintained and policed those boundaries as they jockeyed for position in the racialized hierarchy at the school. However, I will also show that, perhaps as a result of the friendships that existed among them, in some cases students deconstructed traditional racial boundaries and allowed free passage to friends of different racial backgrounds.

Teachers and administrators also took part in boundary work at EA, creating and maintaining boundaries that were not within students' control. Prudence L. Carter (2012) explains that school personnel often construct social boundaries for students based on the conflation of race, ethnicity, gender, or class ascription with academic placement. Caught up in a system of academic tracking that is typical of high schools across the United States, students at EA were often at the mercy of adults who controlled the racialized boundaries inherent in that system. Because decisions about academic placement created unequal educational opportunities for students at EA, the school's tracking practices resulted in insider/outsider status among students and were therefore imbued with social power.

Performing Race

One lazy afternoon during a "flex" study period I witnessed the following scene, recorded in my field notes, among a group of African American females that illustrates racial boundary keeping in action:

> Donna, a substitute teacher, and one of the few African Americans on staff at EA, sits chatting with four African American girls. The conversation gravitates to boys. Adrienne, the only senior in the group, says in amazement, "You know, we only have two black boys in the whole senior class. Two out of forty-two!"
>
> They spend a few minutes naming the cute black boys at the school, and complaining that there aren't more of them. They mention one boy in particular, Henry. Chelsea, asks, "Is he black or does he just look black?"
>
> The other girls glance up in surprise. "What kind of question is that?" asks Keisha from the middle position on the sofa. "If his skin is black, he's black."
>
> Chelsea defends her question. "Well, like, he could be Dominican or something, and have dark skin but not be black."
>
> They agree on this. Keisha, nodding, says "Yeah, that's how it is with my uncle."

Racial identities are produced as race is both discussed and embodied in everyday life (Fine 1997). Children grow up immersed in a racialized social system and therefore construct identities based on the racialized roles they see enacted around them; even preschoolers behave in ways that suggest these roles have already taken hold in their thinking (Van Ausdale and Feagin 2001). What understandings of race did these young women reflect as they explored the question of Henry's blackness? What did it mean to them to be black? Is racial ascription tied to country of origin? Are there specific ways of being and acting that indicate racial background?

While many Americans struggle to define race (Haney López 2000), critical race scholars agree that race is a social construct (Nakkula and Toshalis 2008; Perry 2011); in other words, genetics determines physical appearance, but assigning roles to people based on that appearance is purely a social enterprise. Certainly, the musings of these female students show that, for them, blackness is socially constructed through performance. Henry might look black, but that did not mean he was black; he needed to act in a certain way associated with African Americans in order to be considered black. Although these students were in the process of interrogating blackness and showed some uncertainty as to what, exactly, the criteria for blackness might be, they clearly believed that looking black was not enough to qualify one as being black. Blackness was a quality to be performed.

Performance versus Performativity

Unlike blackness, which must be performed through specific actions to be recognized, whiteness often functions as the invisible norm against which the behaviors of blackness are measured (Beach, Thein, and Parks 2008; Fine 1997; Hollingworth 2009; Marx 2006; Stoughton and Sivertson 2005; Trainor 2008). David Gillborn (2009) explains that the word "performance" implies that the actor is aware that he or she is performing. In the case of whites, this is largely not true since whites have normalized their position of dominance and its accompanying social power. For whites, the expression of racial identity might be more aptly classified as "performativity" because, as dominant social players, their "identities are strengthened and legitimized through countless acts of reiteration and reinforcement" (55). Thus, white students are not aware of how their behaviors could be characterized in racial terms. This naturalized performativity gives whiteness "its deep-rooted, almost invisible status" (56) that forms the backdrop upon which African American students' appearance and behaviors stand out (Youdell 2004). So, at EA, whereas white students' racial identity was submersed in an invisible performativity, African American students expressed racial identity through performance of quintessentially "black" ways of looking, talking, and being, of which they and others were continually aware. The following descriptions will show how students' everyday behaviors embodied race and helped maintain the racial boundary keeping that was prevalent at the school.

Looking the Part

The school's strict uniform and dress policy made it difficult to determine how students expressed identity through dress, but the clothing regulations at EA modeled the preppy look that, Bucholtz (2011) notes, "traditionally designates a clean-cut conservative style . . . associated with inherited wealth and privilege" (91) and, by extension, whiteness. Students at EA were required to wear polo shirts (tucked in) and khakis. According to the student handbook, hoodies and "excessively loose clothing" were banned at all times. Baggy clothing has been associated with hip-hop culture (and, to a large extent, blackness) for years, and is viewed negatively and even criminalized in some places through "anti-sagging ordinances" (Perry 2011, 173) that make showing boxers beneath loose fitting, baggy pants a misdemeanor. Since EA advertises itself as a college preparatory school, it comes as no surprise that the school's strict dress code forced all students into dressing in the traditional preppy style that is common among uniform-wearing academic institutions, and I do not mean to imply that if not for the school dress code all black students would favor hip-hop fashion styles any more than all white students would wear preppy-style clothing. Black and white students come from a variety of cultural backgrounds and express identity through dress in a variety of ways. However, EA's dress code reinforced whiteness as the invisible standard of normative dress and sent the clear message that a dress style associated with an element of black youth culture was not appropriate on school grounds.

Gimme a Head with Hair

Students had little freedom to alter their dress at EA, but they could and did express identity through their choice of hairstyle. The shaggy look was definitely "in" among many of the white boys, and seemed to coincide with interest in science fiction and video games, activities that earned one the designation of "nerd." Many of the members of the Gamers Club (populated by the male "nerds") sported this longer, shaggy hairstyle.

Other white males had traditional short hair or buzz cuts. Several of the boys in Joann's classes played sports (the "jocks"), and they all wore their hair very short. At one point the white members of the baseball team began to grow "Mohawk" hairstyles: buzzed around the sides with a strip of longer hair growing down the middle. Rob, a member of this group, told me that the hairstyle was a "thing" the team was doing to imitate their coach, a young white male. Almost all of the African American males I came in contact with wore their hair short and sometimes brushed it during class (something I never saw a white male do). Dan, an African American tenth grader, wore long cornrowed braids for a while but eventually cut them off and kept his hair short after that.

Hairstyles for females varied and, as might be expected, represented complicated identity choices. For white girls the most popular hairstyle by far was long, straight, and silky, sometimes worn back in a ponytail, but more often down and flowing. A few African American girls wore cornrows or beaded braids, but this style was not very common. Many wore their hair pulled back in tight ponytails or buns and held in place with clips and headbands (à la 2012 Olympic gold medalist Gabby Douglas, whose choice of this hairstyle stirred up controversy on social media sites). Some wore their straightened hair down—I walked into the ladies' room one morning and saw two African American girls straightening their hair with a flat iron before classes started—and others wore weaves, hair extensions, or wigs.

One day Carrie, a white female student who usually wore her wavy, blond-highlighted hair up in a bun, appeared with her hair straightened and down. The response from the other girls was immediate. Susan (also white, with long, silky brown hair) and Rihanna (a black student who changed her look often with long, silky hair extensions) ran over to Carrie, squealing, "Your hair is so cute!" and "I didn't know your hair was so long!" Both girls stroked Carrie's hair for several minutes until they were required to sit down for the start of class. I spent many hours watching white girls run their fingers through their hair during classes, something the African American girls who wore wigs, weaves, extensions, or who straightened their hair with chemical relaxers did as well.

Neal A. Lester (2000) describes the importance of hairstyle in African American identity, going so far as to state that the "implications and consequences of the seemingly radical split between European standards of beauty and black people's hair become ways of building or crushing a black person's self-esteem, all based on the straightness or nappiness of an individual's hair" (203). As a white woman, I cannot pretend to understand the complexities of hair for African American females, or what the primacy of the long, silky, and sometimes blond look among the black girls at EA said about their racial identity. Although in eleventh grade honors class we discussed the damage that internalizing white beauty standards did to the characters in *The Bluest Eye*, ironically, we never talked about how this same internalization might be reflected in hairstyle choice for modern African American women or for the African American girls in the class. We simply didn't go there. Instead, we skirted the issue and failed to challenge students' statements that normalized whiteness as the standard of beauty.

As an outsider, I questioned my right to comment on the subject. In retrospect, thinking about what hair meant to the black girls in Joann's classes may provide more insight into my own racial identity than into theirs. The truth is that both Joann and I avoided commenting when African American girls changed their hairstyles, pretending we did not notice the dramatic transformations that took place almost before our eyes. Perhaps this is understandable on Joann's part, although I found her claim that she did not notice when African American girls went from dark hair to blond and back to dark again in the span of forty-eight hours, or grew silky, shoulder-length hair overnight, a bit hard to believe. My own hesitancy in addressing the topic with students, even casually, was much more difficult for me to understand. Here I was, a researcher whose work was meant to problematize colorblind ideology, pretending to be colorblind when it came to black girls' hair, acting as if these girls were members of a secret club that I dare not enter or even acknowledge. Perhaps I sensed the struggle that Lester (2000) describes within the ranks of black girls and women over what constitutes "good hair" and how to achieve it. Perhaps I feared that attention to African American hairstyles from a white woman would exoticize the students, somewhat akin to Lester's first white roommate who asked to touch his hair and was surprised that it "did not feel like steel wool" (202). Or, perhaps my own unexamined fear that pointing out differences in physical appearance based on race might result in accusations of racism stopped me from chatting about hair with the African American girls. For whatever reason, I had created a racial boundary between myself and the students in the form of self-imposed silence over the topic of hair.

Ironically, it was the students themselves who eventually shattered this boundary. One morning toward the end of the school year, students had been assigned to work on their "autobiographies," a portfolio project that was meant to sum up the year of academic learning. Cross-racial friendships were evident among the females in the room as they milled around, chatting and laughing while they decorated the three-ring binders that contained their work. I did a double take when Susan and Carrie (both white) walked past me wearing something dark across their foreheads; they were Rihanna's hair extensions, which she had playfully removed and given out to her friends. Susan switched hers to her upper lip as a mustache, and Damara, a black student who had also been a recipient of Rihanna's generosity, glued hers to the front cover of her binder. For the first time I felt the courage to approach the subject of hair with Rihanna. I asked her if the extensions were expensive, and we chatted for a few minutes about the problems she'd had finding a hairdresser who would give her the look she wanted. Joann, who had joined the conversation, seemed surprised to hear that the extensions that Rihanna had worn for weeks, and that were now being passed around the room, were not Rihanna's real hair. Rihanna laughingly chided, "Miss Mitchel, you know what my real hair looks like," and with no self-consciousness she described her real hair under the extensions.

Elizabeth Chin (1999) complicates Lester's (2000) claim that, for African Americans, self-esteem is impacted by a strict good hair / bad hair dichotomy. Finding that poor, urban, African American girls endowed their white dolls with black hairstyles, Chin posits that these girls challenged "constricting notions of race" (315), reshaping racial integration on their own terms. One might argue that African American girls at EA performed similar boundary work through the use of hair extensions and wigs, and that their willingness to play with these racial boundaries by passing out hair extensions in class signifies their awareness of, as Chin describes, "the socially constructed nature of race, the ambiguity of a racialized existence, and the flexibility of racialized expression" (316). Rihanna's literal play with her hair extensions represented her symbolic boundary work in two ways. First, as Chin suggests of the girls with whom she worked, Rihanna broadened her racial identity past the traditional strictures of the racial discourse surrounding the good hair/bad hair dichotomy, in so doing establishing a position of power by refusing the boundaries that discourse implies. Second, by handing out her hair extensions to her white friends, Rihanna allowed them entrance into her boundary work/play. Because of these friendships she allowed a traditional boundary (expressed by the well-known axiom, "never mess with a black woman's hair") to be permeable rather than fixed.

Acting the Part

While physical appearance was an important way for students at EA to express racial identity, it was through their actions that racial identity took concrete form. Through everyday behaviors, students placed themselves in clearly defined racial categories that were recognized by their peers.

Seating by Race

At EA it was common for African American and white students to sit separately during classes, lunch period, and special events. A few white students consistently crossed this visual boundary, but for the most part self-segregation prevailed. In Joann's classes this was not always easy to achieve, since she would often assign seats based on either academic level or behavioral issues. Students would follow her prescribed seating pattern for a day or two but then would count on her forgetting the new arrangement and go back to sitting where they pleased. Usually, this strategy worked.

Even among the self-proclaimed friendships of the eleventh grade honors class, students usually sat not only according to race but according to color, as light-skinned African American and Asian students tended to sit with whites and dark-skinned African Americans usually sat together. Gender, too, was a factor in students' seating choices, but for some students race trumped gender when it came to choosing a seat. For example, Michael, an African American male, always sat at a table with Latina and African American females during homeroom, but at other times during the day was found almost exclusively in the company of other African American males. Edward, a white eleventh grader, always sat with white females and never with the African American males in his class.

Students' self-segregated seating choices, a common occurrence in racially diverse settings (Pettigrew 2012), were another way that friendships at EA complicated a traditional racial boundary. Tatum (1997) views self-segregation by African American students in mixed-race settings as a "developmental process in response to an environmental stressor, racism" (62). She believes that for African American students in racially mixed schools, self-actualized racial identity depends on connecting with other African American students during the school day. During our interview, Anthony, an African American student, confirmed Tatum's claim. Although he was friendly with many white students, Anthony told me that he felt a "divide" existed between black and white students, and explained the tendency to self-segregate: "We see things the same way. We act the same way. We understand . . . not saying that they [white students] can't, it's just that they usually don't." Perhaps to ensure a sense of emotional comfort or safety, Anthony needed to connect with students who thought and acted like he did and, therefore, understood him. While he valued his friendships with whites, he also needed to socialize with students with whom he could most identify.

However, Anthony's experience differs from Tatum's (1997) explanation of self-segregation in a significant way. Tatum suggests that racial clustering may be a sign of oppositional identity (Fordham and Ogbu 1986). In contrast, Anthony's reflection that, while it is possible for white students to "understand" African American students ("it's not that they *can't*"), this understanding is usually not present ("they usually *don't*") puts the responsibility for the racial divide he perceives on the shoulders of the white students and on the academic structures that kept students racially segregated. Anthony explained, "In our school in general, most of the white kids are in excelled classes and most of the black kids are in unexcelled classes, so there's not much time . . . to get to know each other." Therefore, it is white students' lack of understanding along with academic tracking structures that, in Anthony's mind, are responsible for self-segregation at school, not African American students' need to declare opposition to the dominant white culture.

Mary E. Thomas (2011), who studied girls' racial and gender identity at an urban school after a painful "race riot" between Hispanic and Armenian students had taken place, cautions against ignoring the damage of the racialization processes that lurk beneath students' self-segregation. She points out that the way students use space at school reflects their segregated experience outside of school, an experience steeped in past racist policies. Viewing self-segregation at school as a step in the journey toward racial self-actualization, as Tatum (1997) does, ignores both the painful history of racism and the present pain of racialized exclusion that students of color face both inside and outside of school. Although some white EA students insisted that neighborhoods and public schools are segregated due to individual choice, their lack of awareness does not change the fact that racially segregated suburbs throughout the United States, including those that surround EA, are the product of past and present racist housing policies and practices (Anacker 2010; Logan 2011; Meyer 2000; Seitles 1998), and that their self-segregation at school may be a reflection of those policies.

In some schools, racial self-segregation among students takes on an exclusionary and even threatening nature (Shankar 2008; Tatum 1997; Thomas 2011). This was not the case at EA; there the lines of self-segregation were visible but easily penetrable. Teachers at EA did not perceive their students' segregated seating choices as threatening and did nothing to intervene.[1]

Since there was nothing menacing or hostile about the behavior of the students at this friendly school, there was no need for teachers to notice or think deeply about students' self-segregation. Students did cluster racially but milled around freely with none of the threatening looks, racial epitaphs, or other types of harassment among students described at other schools (Perry 2002; Thomas 2011). From what I observed, there were no out-of-bounds physical spaces for students of any background. However, the same was not true of the boundaries that protected other racialized behavioral patterns at the school.

Nerds and Jocks

High school students have taken part in identity groupings for decades, with race often influencing group ascription in unspoken ways (Kendall 2011; Perry 2002; Tyson 2011). Perhaps because of its small size and suburban location, the only two identity groups that students consistently mentioned at EA were "nerds" and "jocks." Highly visible in popular culture, both of these groups represent stereotypes that are especially problematic for male students. The male nerd is often portrayed in movies and on TV as white, unpopular, unsociable, and the antithesis of masculinity. Male nerds are associated with high intelligence and computer savvy (Kendall 2011) but are often socially devalued by other students and at risk for exclusion (Rentzch, Schütz, and Schröder-Abé 2011). The nerd's opposite is the African American "gangsta," portrayed as dangerous in his unbridled masculinity. These highly racialized depictions of male identity represent undesirable caricatures that can damage the social placement of both white and black male students, albeit in different ways. Males thought of as nerds may be avoided as social outcasts, whereas gangstas might be avoided because they are viewed as threatening and dangerous. Jock identity is also problematic for males, often accompanied by "homophobia, alcohol and substance abuse, risky sexual behavior, and other psychological conflicts" (Harris and Struve 2009, 4). In spite of the damaging aspects of these identities, nerds and jocks live on in the media and in high schools across the country. However, perhaps due to the school's friendly ethos, I did not witness the hostility that others report are common between these groups (Bishop et al. 2004).

Not surprisingly, group membership for nerds and jocks at EA largely maintained traditional racial boundaries. The jocks, members of the school's sports teams, were for the most part divided racially; African Americans dominated the basketball team while the soccer, baseball, and softball teams were made up mostly of white players. The nerds were exclusively white or Asian, described by students as "smart," "into books," "into computers," and "artsy."

Other than the members of the Gamers Club (who were all male), the most visible group of nerds among the students I knew at EA were white and Asian females, whose gender placed them at lower risk for social isolation than their male counterparts (Rentzch, Schütz, and Schröder-Abé 2011). Rather than facing exclusion by their peers, these students exerted a form of social and academic power that sometimes results from identity group memberships (Perry 2002) because of their "artsy" persona; their work on the many visual projects that Joann assigned and displayed in the classroom stood out for its creativity and aesthetic quality.

B.K., a white female and self-proclaimed jock, described these female nerds in this way:

> So they're really artsy, they're all so very artistic. It makes me, like, I'm in all their classes, and they get assigned an art project, and I'm like [groans, puts head down as if deflated] and they're like, oooh! [raises arms as if ecstatic]. And I'm like, oh [groans, lowers head again]. . . . And um, they're all like, love each other. They're best friends, and they have all the same classes together, which is the honors class, so, if you want to categorize them into the "nerds" or something, that's what they would be categorized to.

The female "artsy nerds" described here were a confident and socially powerful group at EA, able to deflate students like B.K. because of the esteem their artistic talent won them.

In spite of the racial segregation that existed among students in these cliques, students at EA often naturalized racial group divisions, claiming that students grouped together based on personalities or interests and that race was not a factor in identity groupings (Carter 2012; Thomas 2011). When

I asked students during interviews if groups like the nerds fell along racial lines, I was consistently met with blank stares, and then denial that race played a part in these alliances. Radha, a South Asian student and a member of the "artsy nerds," admitted that there were "racial cliques" in "public schools," but not at her school. She attributed this to the fact that, in her words, "There isn't much diversity here, I think." When I pointed out that EA is much more racially diverse than the surrounding public schools, including the school that Radha had previously attended, she seemed genuinely surprised, telling me that she had not noticed that. Nakia, a black student, explained that school "cliques" formed based on the neighborhoods students came from. She said, "It makes sense, 'cause like you live together so you play together and you come here together." Likewise, Jada, an African American student, said of student groupings, "It doesn't have to do with race, but people who are into stuff that . . . they're into, they'll group up." Even Joann tended to naturalize students' segregated seating choices: when I pointed out to her how students in her homeroom racially self-segregated, she was surprised, saying she had never noticed and had always assumed that students sat together according to interests, "like Dungeons and Dragons," she said. The racialized aspect of her assumption—Dungeons and Dragons is largely a white, "nerd," phenomenon—did not occur to her.

Coolness

According to Bucholtz (2011), nerds are the "hyperwhite" (140) opposite of cool. She describes African American students, though, as "cool almost by definition" (45); even those African American students who do not adopt the gangsta persona (Kendall 2011) are positioned at the top of the coolness chain in a setting where coolness is a desired commodity (Bucholtz 2011). Richard Majors (2001) describes the development of the "cool pose" in black males as a response to "an externally imposed invisibility" (211). He explains that for black men, the adopting of the cool persona is a response to the limitations they have experienced as the targets of racism. Therefore coolness is an alternate means of gaining social power for African American males. C. J. Pascoe (2007) found that among males at a mixed-race high school, the dreaded designation "fag," the very antithesis of coolness, was highly racialized. African American males were able to engage in behaviors that might earn their white counterparts "fag identity" (72) because their coolness protected them from such verbal attacks.

The same social hierarchy surrounding coolness existed among some males at EA, in spite of the friendly environment. Tom, a white tenth grader, stated during our interview that it was "harder to be cool" if you were white. At EA, as at other schools (Kromidas 2012; Pascoe 2007), students contrasted coolness with whiteness, and Tom was not happy about this arrangement. He saw coolness as a status to be desired and did not appreciate his possible exclusion from the cool category because of his racial ascription. For Tom, coolness at EA was infused with the reverse racism discourse since he clearly believed that his whiteness caused him an unfair disadvantage in social placement. Tom, who travels to school each day with many African American students, illustrated his point by describing what he perceived as the victimization of whites on the school bus:

> TOM: But, you know, I'm not trying to be racist in the Rosa Parks way, but you know, the back of the bus used to be the bad thing, and now the back of the bus is the cool thing. . . . So who sits in the back, who speaks up, you know if, actually on my bus, generally, the African American people, if they speak up to someone who's white, it's fine. But if someone who's white speaks up, then they're ignorant, they're, you could go as far as being called racist.
>
> M: And what do you mean by "speak up"?
>
> T: . . . Speak up for equality . . . like, I deserve to sit here just as much as the next person.

Like other white students I spoke with, Tom begins his statement with the "I'm not trying to be racist" disclaimer, perhaps fearing that the mere mention of race leaves him open to this accusation. He then follows by mentioning Rosa Parks, the African American woman who in 1955 refused to give up her seat at the front of the bus for a white person. From the context of our conversation I believe that, ironically, Tom identifies himself with Parks as the victim of discrimination, which, for Tom, takes place on two levels. Not only is Tom denied access to coolness by his exclusion from the back of the bus because he is white, but if he decides to "speak up for equality" (as Parks did) he runs the risk of being accused of racism. African Americans, says Tom, are allowed to "speak up," but he, as a white person, is not. Tom's racial identity is infused with a power struggle over possession of a highly sought-after coolness status. Further, Tom, like other students at EA, believes that whites are more restricted in what they can do or say because African Americans use accusations of racism to gain unfair advantage over whites.

Although they were not in the same class or grade level, Anthony confirmed Tom's dualistic construction of white versus cool during a class discussion about discrimination. Edward, a white student, had argued that "all people have experienced discrimination in some form." Naturalizing racism, Edward continued, "If you're a minority among a group of others who are the majority, discrimination is just natural." Anthony agreed with Edward, saying, "Some people may think they're the only cool ones, and if you're not like them you're not cool." Anthony did not specifically refer to African American students as the "some people" who think they're "the only cool ones," but within the context of the discussion the implication was clear. Anthony's example positions whites as the victims of discrimination at the hands of "cool" blacks. Thus, by inhabiting "coolness" as their exclusive property, African American students constructed a racial identity that granted them social power over whites.

Going to "Choych"

African American students often performed their "coolness" with classroom behaviors designed to entertain themselves and the students around them. One category of such behaviors involved religious expression. Many students talked about attending religious services at their temples, synagogues, or churches, and a few told me that their fathers were pastors. According to data from the National Survey of Youth and Religion, African Americans are, by several measures, the most religious group of teens in the country (Christerson, Edwards, and Flory 2010). White and Latino youth also expressed a high level of religious belief, but African American youth engaged in more religious practice than their white and Latino counterparts, including church attendance, Bible reading, and prayer; this engagement was reflected in the behavior of African American students at EA. The saying, often attributed to Dr. Martin Luther King Jr., that eleven A.M. on Sunday is the most segregated hour of the week, holds true for many of the churches that surround the Excellence Academy area. Therefore, in a society that has racialized religion, it is not surprising that religious expression serves as a way for some youth to perform racial identity. I found that many black students regularly mimicked religious expression for the sake of humor, sometimes among themselves, and other times in front of the class.

I first began to wonder about the role of religious mimicry by African American students on the morning the eleventh grade on-level class presented their "American Dream Quilt" squares, part of a project from *The Great Gatsby* unit. The "quilt" was made of pictures students had found on the Internet to represent their ideas of the American Dream and captioned with a quote of their choosing from Fitzgerald's novel. Students were told to share their idea of the American Dream before pinning their picture to the board. Following is an excerpt from my field notes:

> Samar, an African American male, stands in front of the noisy class, waiting for quiet. Rihanna calls out, "Everybody at choych say amen!" Several students, all African American, respond with a loud, "Amen!" Jolene closes her eyes and raises her right hand in mock worship, then perks up and asks excitedly, "What if everybody did church?"
>
> Next, Kala (African American female) stands to share her quilt, a painting of a grassy field. "Love doesn't have any race, color or religion," she says.
>
> "That's right!" exclaims Rihanna. She puts her head down in her arms, making believe she's crying. "Choych! Choych!" she calls out several times.

Rihanna's shouts of "Choych! Choych!" and Jolene's raising of hands in simulated worship are examples of the mock religious expression among African American students that I witnessed many times at EA.

Violet and Juliette, African American eleventh graders, often pretended to be singing in a church choir, at times joined by Karla (also African American) and Dana (white); once they launched into a soulful version of "Amazing Grace" during group work, but stopped when they couldn't remember all of the words. When class ended that morning, Juliette and Violet picked up again as they left the room, singing, "Amazing Gra-ay-ay," holding the notes in an exaggerated way. During the unit on *The Crucible*, Joann told the class that reciting "The Lord's Prayer" was a way for those accused of witchcraft to prove their innocence during the Salem witch hunts. Violet, who was standing up at the board, immediately recited the prayer in full, to the giggles of those around her. During the same unit, Joann asked the class to define the word "theocracy." Violet replied with the words, "the Lort," an expression made famous through the comic religious mimicry of Tyler Perry's Madea character. At other times I heard African American students jokingly tell each other, "You need to pray!" or say of themselves, "I need the Lord!" One day Jada rushed into the room between classes, looking for a book she had left behind. When she found it inside a desk, she declared a loud "Thank you, Jesus!" to the surprise of the white boys sitting at the table. Another day, Jada thanked me for providing pizza for her class by saying dramatically, "Mrs. Modica, you are the blessed savior! You are the blessed favored one!" She then went on to describe how hungry she was because of the terrible lunch served in the cafeteria earlier that day.

Dana, an eleventh grader, was the only white student who participated in the mock religious role-plays or overt religious comments that I observed among African American students. Early on in my fieldwork I had noticed Dana's friendship with Juliette, Violet, and Karla, all African American females. Dana often jokingly imitated church members with them, pretending to clap offbeat or play a percussion instrument incorrectly (i.e., blowing on a triangle instead of hitting it). When I mentioned this friendship to Joann, she said that Dana was "completely accepted by them" (meaning the African American girls). Joann also told me that Dana had a reputation for "only dating black guys," saying that she had heard Dana admit to this herself. One day I observed Dana teaching a Christian children's song to Juliette, Violet, and Karla. It was a song that I was familiar with from my days as a Sunday school teacher in white churches. The words were:

I am a C
I am a C-H
I am a C-H-R-I-S-T-I-A-N
And I have C-H-R-I-S-T
In my H-E-A-R-T
And I will L-I-V-E E-T-E-R-N-A-L-L-Y!

Dana sang this to her friends so quickly, clapping and patting her legs in rhythm, that if I had not been familiar with the song I would not have been able to decipher the words. As she ended, all of them burst into giggles, and Dana explained laughingly, "It's what we white folks sing in church." While meant as a joke, Dana's explanation served the purpose of acknowledging and respecting the racial boundary that existed between her and her African American friends. She related to and connected with their religious practice yet, as a member of a white church, differentiated it from her own.

Talking and Rapping Black

Black students also performed race through the use of Black English (also known as African American Language, Ebonics, or African American Vernacular English). Words and phrases like, "Sup?" "Jawn," "Gangsta," "Where she at?" "I ain't got none," or "She be talking" were common, especially when teachers weren't listening. John Ogbu (2004) notes, "after emancipation, Blacks were required to behave and talk the way White people actually behaved and talked" (14). Accordingly, the language expectation at EA established whiteness as the standard; the "Classroom Norm" requiring students to "use *formal conventions* for ALL oral and written responses" was posted on the wall for all to see. With these directions looming, it is easy to understand why the students who were most likely to speak in Black English almost always switched back to "formal conventions" when talking to teachers. African American students in the honors classes tended more toward standard grammatical forms, but on occasion they, too, used Black English when talking quietly with one another.

Carter (2012) views school policies that privilege white modes of language and behavior as "organizational (in)flexibility that bars reciprocity in cultural exchanges among students within schools" (13). Such policies and practices construct symbolic boundaries among students, creating outsider status and, therefore, the lack of belonging for students whose home cultural language and behaviors fall outside of the white cultural "classroom norms." At EA, students' performances of blackness stood outside the norm because of school policies that insisted on white behavioral standards. Therefore, the teachers and administrators who maintained these policies, posting them on classroom walls, were partly responsible for turning cultural practices into racial performance boundaries among students. By affirming white cultural language as the classroom norm, teachers and administrators designated all other cultural behaviors as unacceptable and undesirable, contributing to a school and classroom climate that privileged whiteness (Carter 2012; Ochoa and Pineda 2008).

African American students were also likely to perform race during their down times (often before class officially started but sometimes during group work) with impromptu raps, sometimes accompanied by drum beating on the desks and chair dancing. Teachers were usually quick to put a stop to the fun, but now and then, if they were distracted with other things, the spontaneous performances would continue for several minutes, gaining in enthusiasm as they did. Many white students looked on, smiling, and a few participated, but for the most part these musical performances were owned by the African American students, and it was this behavior that partly earned them "cool" status among their peers. Thus, at EA, race was performed daily through the complex interaction of physical appearance and overt behaviors that distinctly aligned students with white or black identity status.

Policing the Borders

Discussions of "acting white" and "acting black" were common at EA, both in class conversations and during my interviews with students. I first heard African American students talk about "acting white" as they discussed *The Scarlet Letter*. As a means of exploring the social "labeling" that takes place in the novel, Joann asked students to record on one side of a sticky note the labels they felt others placed on them, and on the other side, the labels they placed on themselves. Most of the students in the class focused on personality traits like "funny" or "shy," but table four, populated mostly by African American girls, chose to label themselves by race. On the side of the sticky note that was meant to depict how others labeled her, Juliette wrote, "acts like white girl, Oreo." I asked Juliette why she thought people said that about her. She explained, "I used to go to an all-white school, and so people said I act like a white girl."

"What does a white girl act like?" I asked. Juliette shrugged. "I don't talk a lot, I talk nicely, I dress nice," she said. Violet volunteered that she and her cousins were often told that they "act like white girls" for the same reasons. Juliette and Violet's experiences reflect the policing of racial performance borders by African American youth as they challenge their peers for deviating from the cultural norm of speaking in Black English (Erickson 1987; Winkler 2012).

During our interview, Ryan, a female African American student, stated that it was common for students to accuse others of acting white or acting black. She believed that students are "forced" into friendship groups based on physical appearance (i.e., racial category) even if their personalities are dissimilar. Ryan explained the repercussions students faced for too much white/black boundary crossing in their friendship groups:

RYAN: I think it's something that people accept eventually. At first it's uncomfortable because you know, people don't just let it go at first. They, like, make sure that everyone knows about it, and make sure that everyone puts their opinion out about it, you know what I mean? Nothing is ever a secret. Everything is always out in the open [laughs].

MM: [laughs] Everybody knows everything about everybody.

R: [laughing] Yes, yes.

M: And that can be hard sometimes.

R: Although, I mean, but with that, it's like, you get everything out at one time. You know, everyone knows, so eventually tomorrow I can, I can move on from it. But today, everyone gonna, [laughs] everyone's gonna know, everyone's gonna approach you about it.

Ryan describes how policing racial boundaries functions: cross-racial friendships may be accepted tomorrow, but not without scrutiny today. These friendships, while eventually accepted, are also the fodder of public commentary and critique among students.

Later in our interview, Ryan revealed her belief that blacks face more rigid behavioral expectations than whites. She stated:

I feel like as soon as an African American person walks into a room they're categorized, their whole entire life is just spilled out in front of them because everyone already knows their entire, you know, their struggles and everything. But for a white person it's not like that. I mean, I feel like people give them a chance to, you know, tell about themselves and, you know, paint their own picture. I feel like for African American people it's painted.

Ryan feels that as an African American she lacks the opportunity or the power to "paint her own picture": to present herself to the outside world in whatever unique way she might choose. In her view, her blackness creates expectations about her that she cannot escape.

Another African American student, Nakia, also felt that she had been pigeonholed by racial performance expectations that existed at the school. She said, "I used to have a clique with the smart people and stuff, and they're white." Because of these friendships, she said, "the black kids" would accuse her of acting white. Nakia told me: "We've all experienced it, like some way or another, where [laughs] someone would be like, tell a white person, stop acting black, or somebody will tell a black person, stop acting white, like, that's kind of like a racial slur." It's not clear whether it was Nakia's association with white students in and of itself that brought about the sanctioning she received, or if it was her black peers' recognition of white students as "the smart people" that earned Nakia their disapproval. What is clear is that, her laughter notwithstanding, Nakia perceives this peer sanctioning to be a form of racism. Her analysis, "that's kind of like a racial slur" may suggest that she felt degraded (as someone called a racial slur would) when she came under the scrutiny of black students for supposedly acting white.

B.K. also connected the policing of racial performance boundaries with racism. She said, "I think that both black and white people are racist, like 'Stop acting so white,' like, 'Why are you trying to act black?'" In B.K.'s view, policing the borders of racial performance is, in itself, racist activity because it forces people into, in her words, "definite stereotypes." Further, B.K. believes that questioning the acting white / acting black boundary is risky. She says: "I think it's not addressed . . . because people try to address it and they get accused of being racist. And like, that's not something you want to be accused of, like, people, you don't want people to think you're racist. It's just not how you want to be seen or viewed." When I asked B.K. what it meant to act white, she explained, "It depends on the person. Like, maybe it's how they're talking, maybe it's what they're doing, what music they listen to, what sports they like." And, according to B.K., for a white person, acting black would consist of "talking weird—not that black people talk weird. . . . Using, um, slang, like that. I don't know, listening to rap music." B.K. confirmed that "anybody" might tell a person to stop acting outside of the prescribed racial norm, and that conversations of this nature are common at EA. "I heard it an hour ago," she said during our interview.

Lucky, an African American male honors student, also emphasized the boundaries of racial behavior during our interview:

MM: Have you ever heard . . . kids talking, saying stuff like, "Oh you're acting white . . ."

LUCKY: [interrupts] Yes.

M: . . . or "Oh you're acting black." You've heard kids say that?

L: Yes.

M: And what's the context? Like, over what kind of things?

L: Like how white people talk, like very proper, like . . . like, a few kids in my class, they talk like they're white. But like, the one Caucasian girl that I'm friends with, she acts like she's black.

M: Mmhmm. And do people say that to her?

L: Yes...And she say, "I know, I'm black."

M: Ok, so she's [laughs]—ok. So, um, so people say it in a teasing way, kind of?

L: No, like, stop acting black. You're not black, you're white.

M: And she says—

L: "No, I'm black."

M: Ok. And so what do people think about that?

L: They don't care. Except for...when she like to take it overboard. Like with some of the words she says. I don't think you know the word we talking about. [pause]

M: You could say it.

L: Nigger.

M: She says that?

L: Yes.

M: And how do people respond when she says it?

L: They, they don't like it when she does that.

M: Yeah. Why not?

L: [pause] 'Cause they feel like she's, I guess, trying too hard, or that, [pause] I don't know. Really, I don't know the reason why, because I don't know why it's not ok for her to say it because she white, but it's ok for us to say it. Because we're black.

M: Mmhmm.

L: I don't know which one is worse...

M: So if you say it, it's ok.

L: Yeah, if I say, "Nigger, please." If she say, "Nigger, please" they would look at her like, "What? Stop saying that, Janie. Like, you not, you not black."

Using Black English at times during the interview, Lucky is clear that his white friend has crossed a firm border in the use of the word "nigger," a word that Lucky believes may be acceptable for African Americans to use but is clearly not for whites. In his view, a certain amount of boundary crossing by this white friend is tolerated, but when she uses a racial slur, approval is withdrawn. Lucky's hesitation to say "nigger" in my presence shows his awareness that its use is not acceptable in every context, and, although he admits that he, too, uses the term, his statement, "I don't know which one is worse," indicates he is not entirely comfortable with its use. Lucky further qualifies his use of the word by saying, "I don't feel like because we're black we ever should get to use that against each other. Like, use that word to each other. Like, it's a form of disrespect." For Lucky, saying "nigger" is within the boundary of acting black, as long as no real disrespect, no use of the word "against each other," is intended. The same is not true for his white friend. When she uses the word she crosses a boundary of acceptable behavior and is pulled back by her friends.

These students' responses show that, despite the friendly atmosphere at EA, racial identity existed within marked behavioral boundaries that were policed by students themselves. Identities such as "nerd," "jock," and "cool" held unspoken racialized meanings, and membership in these groups provided students with insider status and power. The white and Asian "artsy nerds" maintained academic and social power through their tight-knit friendships and artistic abilities. African American students reversed the traditional black/white power differential (Tyson 2011), gaining social power through their "cool" status and perhaps, as Carter (2005) found, gaining a sense of belonging and self-worth by protecting group membership from outside intrusion. In response, Tom, a white student, sought to regain power by positioning whites as the new victims of racism, excluded from coolness and, ironically, able to identify with Rosa Parks as targets of discrimination. Lucky protected his racial identity by policing the racial language boundary. For him, the ability to use the word "nigger" represented insider status, and although he was not sure if his use of the word was acceptable, he was sure that use of the word by his white friend, an outsider, was not. As one of the only African American male honors students in the school, Lucky's use of the insider term may have been especially important to him; although he was in the "smart" classes with the white students, his friends could rest assured that in this regard, Lucky acted black.

Racial Performance and Academic Achievement

As students performed the work of racial boundary keeping, the institution also worked to maintain racial boundaries through its academic tracking practices. For decades scholars have debated how separating students based on academic performance affects racial identity and future school achievement. Some have argued that African American students develop an oppositional identity and reject good grades to avoid accusations of acting white (Fordham and Ogbu 1986; Tatum 1997); while it is not necessarily the grades themselves they want to avoid, students relate the thinking and acting that leads to good grades with whiteness (Ogbu 2004). Others argue that many African American and Latino students do not succeed academically not to avoid accusations of acting white but because they are not welcomed into an educational system that privileges whiteness (Carter 2005), and they point out that students learn to connect race and academic status through continued exposure to racially patterned class divisions at school, not in their home communities (Tyson 2011). As in many other school environments, academic tracking practices at EA influenced the racialized academic boundaries students experienced every day.

Students' Perspectives

Outwardly, students at EA did not equate academic achievement with acting white, insisting that ascription to racial performance categories had more to do with membership in friendship groups and cultural styles expressed through language and music. For example, when I asked Ryan if people might say a person was acting white because of academic achievement, she responded hesitantly, "Um, I've never, I've never seen that. But, I have seen it, like, as far as the way people talk or dress, who they hang out with, what they watch, what they listen to. Um, I've seen it in that way." However, in more subtle ways students confirmed that race and academic achievement were, in fact, related.

During our interview, Lucky denied that acting white is equated with academic achievement, but as this interview segment shows, he was ambivalent about the subject:

MM: Ok, so, um, has anybody ever been accused of acting white because they're smart, or in honors classes?

LUCKY: Mmm, no. Like, all my classes are, like literally, all my classes are honors. They don't like, "Oh you act white," or . . .

M: Nobody's ever said that?

L: No.

M: So it's only about kind of talk, slang expressions . . .

L: Yeah, I feel like, 'cause, because you're white, you're smart, because you're black, you're dumb.

M: You don't feel like that, or you do?

L: I do feel like that.

M: You do feel like that?

L: Yeah. Like how, like they was talking about, remember the day we was talking about in class like, like, people from Carltonville, . . .

M: Yeah.

L: . . . or like, they're like, the black people are mostly focused on athletics, whereas the white people are focused on school, which is why when they come here, the black people are in all the normal classes and the white people are in the honors classes . . .

M: Yeah. So then I'm trying to understand your answer then. Do people think that if you're smart, it's like you're acting white?

L: No, not my friends.

M: So nobody's ever said that to you . . .

L: No.

M: . . . but there is kind of this underlying kind of theme that the honors classes are mostly white kids, or . . .

L: Which they are.

M: . . . or Asian.

L: They're mostly white or Asian, and they're mostly female.

M: Yes. Right, ok. And so people are aware of that, kind of.

L: Yes.

I include this interview segment in its entirety to show my trouble at getting to the crux of Lucky's meaning. Was he or wasn't he saying that he and his peers view academic achievement as acting white? Perhaps Lucky himself is unsure of how his position as an honors student affects his racial identity. If acting black involves use of Black English and identification with black cultural styles, then Lucky acts black. But if acting white involves placement in honors classes, then Lucky acts white. Lucky seems to be saying that although his black friends have never accused him, personally, of acting white, they are aware that white and Asian students mostly populate the honors classes. Therefore, among these students whiteness was associated with academic achievement, but crossover into academic success for students like Lucky was allowed and maybe even coveted by his African American friends.

Anthony, an African American honors student, also both affirmed and denied that race was linked to academic success:

MM: Some kids have talked about this whole notion of acting white, . . .

ANTHONY: [interrupting] Oh, yeah!

M: . . . and acting black. That, that comes up a lot . . .

A: Yeah

M: . . . among students. In what ways does it come up, in your, from your perspective?

A: So, let's see. Acting white is more, uh, not being studious, but kind of like, studying all the time, the nerd, the, uh, being in the house, not going to parties, and just, the way you talk also. Like, you laugh at different things, like, you don't listen to a certain kind of music. Like if you listen to, like, country, or that pop stuff, like Lady, not Lady, yeah, no, not really Lady GaGa . . . like, like, the bands, like One Direction, like all that goes into acting white. So like, I know, my best friend is criticized all the time for acting white.

M: Because of the music she likes.

A: Because of the music she likes, how she acts, like the, even the clothes she wears!

M: And so she's criticized by black kids?

A: Yeah! . . . Mmhmm . . . definitely. I mean, like with me, I guess you can say I don't really get teased for acting white, but I get teased because I am black. I don't act white, but I have white friends. And I am in classes with white people.

M: 'Cause you're in honors classes.

A: Exactly. So I don't really, you know what I mean? I don't really have, I don't have that, I don't act that way? But, I, I guess, it's because I'm still there.

M: Yeah. Right, because of who you associate with.

A: Yeah.

M: And is it kind of a good-natured teasing? Or is it . . .

A: [interrupts] Nah, no, definitely not.

M: [laughs] It's not good-natured? It's, like, serious?

A: No, not serious. It's like, "Oh man, he's gonna go to his white friends. Just, just go ahead."

Like Lucky, Anthony demonstrates ambivalence in his understanding of the relationship between race and academic achievement. For the most part, he equates acting white with musical taste, clothing style, language, and friendships. However, he also associates acting white with nerdiness and with "not being studious" but "studying all the time." Anthony admits that his black friends tease him not for acting white through speech or cultural styles but for his proximity to white people both in his friendships and because of his academic placement in honors classes (Tyson 2011).

The fact that Lucky and Anthony situate race with academic achievement while denying that they are related speaks to the complexity of the issue for them and other students, and the simultaneous levels on which the ascribing and monitoring of racial identity functions. Students are caught between the performance of race in everyday behaviors, an area that they control, and the school's academic tracking practices that function to segregate students through class placement, an area that is beyond students' jurisdiction.

Samar, an African American male, did not talk with me about racial performance boundaries but made it clear that he equated whiteness with academic achievement through the following scene that took place in class one morning, recorded in my field notes:

> Samar, Chris (both African American), Jack (white), and several other students are working together in a group at table five. The group has chosen Jack as their leader, and Samar does not look happy about this. They begin to banter, Samar making several sarcastic references to Jack's ability to lead. The other group members chat about unrelated topics during this exchange.

> SAMAR: I wish I got good grades like Jack so I could lead. Great leading, Jack.
> JACK: You can lead if you want.
> SAMAR: My skin color stops me from leading.

> Jack looks surprised. He glances at Chris, who is sitting directly opposite him. They both smirk and shake their heads at Samar's words.

> SAMAR: Chris isn't black.
> CHRIS: [surprised] I'm not?

Samar's statement, "my skin color stops me from leading," seemed random at first, but I learned after this incident that Samar was upset because Joann had told him he was failing the class. Samar's words show that he felt his race was connected to his inability to succeed academically. What's more, Samar's barb, "Chris isn't black," is meant as an attack on Chris because of his friendship with Jack (who had recently received school recognition for good grades). During that moment of frustration, Samar claimed that Chris had abandoned his blackness and had gone over to the other side.

Therefore, although students insisted that acting white was not equated with being smart, there was a clear acknowledgment among African American males, in particular, that few of them populated the honors classes; this was a boundary that few were willing or able to cross. Their black friends did not accuse the African American honors students of acting white. These students told me that other black students respected their academic success, looked up to them, and wished they could do the same. Samar equated his skin color with his poor grades in anger; he was upset about his failing grade. The usually self-assured Rihanna put her head down on the desk and cried one day when, as per school policy, Joann would not accept a late homework assignment. Another African American on-level student, Daniel, told me angrily several times that he did not belong in that class and couldn't wait to get back into the honors class. Although Daniel was a high scorer on the PSAT exam (a pretest meant to prepare students for college entrance exams—I saw his scores because he waved them around the room, bragging, when he received them), he lacked the required grades to be placed in the honors class. These students clearly cared about their education. None were discipline problems, and all participated in class discussions with insight and creativity. Yet they were unable or unwilling to meet the requirements of entry into the honors class. Thus, from the perspective of many students, race and academic success were interrelated at EA, and many felt powerless to advance academically the way they wished. Daniel's anger, Rihanna's tears, and Samar's frustration point to this feeling of powerlessness.

Steven Lukes (2005) posits that power functions most effectively when people "accept their role in the existing order of things, either because they can see or imagine no alternative to it, or because they see it as natural and unchangeable" (28). In spite of the frustration African American students at EA showed about their academic status, they seemed at some level to accept their place in lower academic classes; both white and African American students naturalized and took for granted the white/black dichotomy that existed within the academically tracked system (Stoughton and Sivertson 2005). While black students at EA did not avoid academic achievement because they might be accused of acting white, many of them did seem to accept their underrepresentation in honors classes as the natural order of school life, wishing they could achieve but unable to cross the boundary that functioned to keep whites at the top of the school's academic hierarchy.

Anthony described EA's racial/academic reality in this way: "Our vale-dictorian is white, our second in line would be white, and our third, she is, well, Asian, I guess . . . then fourth, white. Fifth, white. Sixth white. Seventh white. I don't think, it goes like eighth and ninth, and then you might, I think they're like right next to each other, they'll be black. And then white, white, white, white, white."

Immersed in a reality that placed whites at the top of a stratified educational system, students made their own meanings regarding the connection between race and academic placement, sometimes accepting the inevitability of their position within that system (MacLeod 2009; Staiger 2005; Tyson 2011).

The Complicity of Adults

Teachers and administrators played a role in policing racial boundaries by naturalizing racialized assumptions about academic ability. Anthony told me that it was standard practice for Linda, an administrator in charge of student placement, to refuse African American males entrance into advanced placement classes before checking their actual grades. He described the following scene between his friend and Linda:

> Yeah, my friend . . . he said, "These are the classes I wanna take."
> And she said, "Uh, I don't know if you're gonna be able to take these classes."
> "Why not?"
> She said, "I just don't know if it's gonna be a good idea." She pulled up his grades, and he has like 3.5, 3.6. She said, "Oh! Really? Wow! I didn't know you were doing this well! That, oh, okay, of course you can take these classes!"

Further, Anthony described how a different African American friend was kept out of the same class:

> He wanted to take an AP class. He, alls you have to do is get a parent's signature, and a teacher's signature. The teacher signed off for the AP class. So he goes downstairs, gets it, and shows her the paper, she pulls up his grades, and then, she's like, "Ahh, you aren't doing bad, but I don't know if you'll be able to handle it." And, he's quieter, so he didn't really stand up for himself, so now he's not gonna take that class, because she said that he couldn't handle it.

Of course, I feel certain that Linda would deny this allegation and insist that class placement is based solely on academic merit. Unfortunately, I did not have the opportunity to interview Linda about the school's placement practices, and I have no way of knowing whether or not Anthony's version of his friend's experience is accurate. I do know, however, that on several occasions Joann and other teachers confirmed to me that there was more leeway in students' academic placement than was admitted to students; because of the smallness of the school and the limited number of classes offered, sometimes grade requirements for higher tracked classes were lifted in order to make students' schedules work. Whether the decision regarding Anthony's friend's placement was just or unjust, it is important to note that Anthony and his friends believed that racial bias existed within the school's academic placement practices.

In another case, teachers and administrators naturalized the racialized hierarchy inherent in academic tracking practices by the curriculum they assigned to the differently tracked classes. Both Joann and Megan (an administrator) confirmed to me that because teachers believed that the on-level students lacked the "maturity" needed to handle the serious nature of the content in *The Bluest Eye* (specifically, incest/rape), only the eleventh grade honors class was allowed to read Morrison's novel; the on-level class was assigned *The Catcher in the Rye* instead. Megan explained:

> I feel like they have the ability to discuss it and be more comfortable with it, because they see it as an author's choice, and not a [pause] shocking crime [smiles]. . . . I'm not saying that—unfortunately, the classes aren't perfectly level, and you're never gonna have—I'm saying maybe some of the on-level students absolutely could read it and experience it, but it was a decision made because of the intense portions of the book. . . . Something that needed that maturity, that it wasn't a joke. . . . It was a decision based off of the fact that we needed to discuss it as intellectual adults, not run around looking at it as pornography.

Megan's response is problematic on a few levels. She acknowledges that the classes (supposedly tracked on the basis of grades alone) are not "perfectly level," admitting that students of varying ability or maturity populate the classes. Her admission contradicts what students are told regarding class placements and gives credence to the suspicions of bias expressed by

Anthony and his friends. Further, even assuming that students are justly placed according to academic merit, in making the decision to keep the on-level class from reading *The Bluest Eye*, teachers and administrators conflated emotional maturity with academic ability in students. Therefore, the on-level students (ironically, the majority of them African Americans) were kept from a text that might stimulate discussion and empower their thinking about important social issues that directly impact their daily lives.

Not only were the students in the on-level class deemed too immature for the text, teachers and administrators believed that their parents, too, were not mature enough to understand the value of this text for their children. While Megan admitted that *The Bluest Eye* was excluded from the on-level curriculum because of fear of parental challenges, Joann was more descriptive in her explanation of the curricular decision:

> My impression is, we can't have parents calling in and complaining. But if you do it with honors kids, their parents can listen to a rationale and respond to that calmly. But if you do it with an on-level kid, it's going to be some uneducated person that calls you up, screaming and cursing at you . . . on voice-mail . . . that's out of control, storms into the building. I mean, there are stories of this, but it's definitely an unsaid prejudice, I think. That on-level kids—I think it's, I guess a class thing.

Students in the eleventh grade on-level class were denied the right to study an important text not because of pedagogical considerations but because of a complicated series of logical missteps that were fueled by race and social class bias. First, the on-level students' academic ability level was conflated with their emotional maturity when it was assumed that these students would, in Megan's words, "run around looking at" *The Bluest Eye* "as pornography." Second, administrators connected the students' academic level with the family's socioeconomic status, which was then seen as an indication of parents' level of education and propensity toward violent reactions. In addition, race is an unspoken factor in this decision because Joann's mention of social class as an explanation for poor parental behavior points to students from the most economically underresourced surrounding areas, which are largely African American. I'm not sure to what extent that type of bias existed among the staff, but certainly it was present; a teacher told me that a school administrator labeled the African American parent of an on-level student as "ignorant" for arguing with teachers about her child's grades. While Joann recognized the class prejudice that informed the decision to keep the Morrison text out of the on-level class, by not mentioning race, she naturalized the racial implications of the decision.

In this way, through naturalized assumptions about students and their parents, teachers and administrators at EA worked to keep the racialized boundary of academic placement secure without ever mentioning race (Staiger 2005; Tyson 2011; Welton 2013). The friendly, harmonious school environment did nothing to protect African American students from biased judgments about them and their families that ultimately limited their educational opportunities. Instead, teachers' perceptions of the racial harmony at the school made thinking about race unnecessary and may have stood in the way of their taking a much needed closer look at the way pedagogical decisions limited the educational experiences of some students.

This chapter has shown that within the friendly environment of EA, students constructed and policed racial performance categories in a struggle to maintain power through social status. At the same time, teachers and administrators granted or denied academic power by preserving the naturalized racialization of academic tracking and by limiting educational opportunities based on misconstrued conflations of race, social class, and emotional maturity. This being the case, one might wonder if the positive effects of the cross-racial friendships that were the source of pride at the school were as far-reaching as they seemed. The safe, calm, friendly environment that prevailed at EA is to be admired and preserved. However, in the midst of this friendly environment, students were both producers and products of racialization processes that perpetuated power structures among them.

2

Anger among Friends

. . . .

Beneath the Surface of
"We All Get Along"

When I asked students and teachers to describe the racial atmosphere at
Excellence Academy, I typically received hearty assurances that "we all get
along here." Some students and teachers favorably compared EA to other
school experiences where there were frequent fights in the hallways or other
overt signs of racial tensions. Juliette, an African American student, said of
her old school in a neighboring white suburb, "People would be disrespect-
ful and talk about my color.... It was very obvious that people didn't like me
because of my skin tone." Juliette was clear that she had never had this experience at EA. In many respects the claim of racial harmony among students
and faculty rang true; the safe, friendly daily atmosphere was an important
characteristic of the school. However, despite the prevalent belief that "we all
get along here," racial identity for students and teachers was nuanced by tensions about race. While students felt comfortable enough with each other to
joke about racial difference, when class discussions of multicultural literature
focused on racial power, privilege, and structural inequity, African American and white students expressed frustration, resentment, and anger at the

marginalization they perceived. White teachers, as well, were anxious and worried about possible student accusations of racism.

This chapter examines the tensions that existed beneath the surface of an outwardly tranquil environment where present-day racial inequity was not often discussed. For both students and teachers, racial identity at EA was infused with feelings of marginalization, victimization, and fear. In the case of one tenth grade class, these feelings flared dramatically during a discussion of the Ishmael Beah's 2007 memoir *A Long Way Gone*.

Getting Along by Making Fun of Race

There is no doubt that the students in Joann's classes were comfortable with each other—so comfortable, in fact, that it was common for them to joke about race and racism. Radha, an Indian student whose close friendship circle included whites and other Asians (the "artsy nerds" that I described in the last chapter), told me laughingly that, "like, no one cares, and if anything we just make fun of, um, race." Students did "make fun" of race in a variety of ways. One day John, a white tenth grader and sometimes class clown, sat next to Marc, an African American student, who was eating a ham sandwich out of a brown paper bag. John began to beg Marc over and over again, "Marc, do you have any crackas? I like crackas, Marc. Do you like crackas?" Marc, smirking, responded, "Why are you so weird?" while the other students at the table laughed. John's joke was as clever as it was comical, since his use of a racial slur, "cracka," was nebulous enough to allow him to cry innocence had Joann overheard him. A student might easily say of someone sitting nearby, "Oh, you give him candy but not me? Are you racist?" The student in possession of the candy might just as easily laugh and toss a piece over.

Sometimes, students used their race joking to make teachers uncomfortable, as when Andrew, an African American male, teased Becca, a white female, by reporting to Joann that Becca had called him a monkey. "Did you?" Joann asked seriously, ready to shift into discipline mode if need be. The usually calm Becca turned bright pink and insisted, "I certainly did not!" and again the students around them, both African American and white, laughed. Ron and James, two white eleventh graders, often shared insider jokes with me about being Italian American and had a standing joke with Joann in which they accused her of being "racist against Italians." Joann usually laughed this off but once in a while reprimanded them, saying they had "gone too far" in their joke. "Someone is going to hear you and take you seriously," she said sternly one of those times.

Alice Pettigrew (2012), who studied secondary students at Kingsland, a British multicultural, urban school, found that despite the staff's disapproval, "the prevalence of racialized language, 'banter,' and joking discourse among and across collective groupings was markedly pronounced" (3). Kingsland students claimed that their freedom to joke about race, even telling racial jokes that some would deem offensive, was evidence that they were not racist. Maria Kromidas (2012) found among elementary-aged children in a multi-racial New York City school that students used humor as a playful means to redefine racial politics. In one particular case, such humor was acceptable in the context of friendship and the student's known antiracist position. Students at EA joked about race, but unlike Kingsland students, they did not tell blatantly racist jokes. At times their jokes about race were made in the context of friendship: Becca and Andrew, for example, always sat at the same table and were obviously friendly during school hours. According to Radha, joking about race among her friends indicated an antiracist stance. She believed that their tendency to "make fun" of race with one another was their way of suggesting that their close friendships would not be marred by racism.

At the same time, playful references to race at EA were not always made within the context of students' friendships, nor were they always indicative of an antiracist stance. John and Marc were not friends, and there was nothing particularly antiracist about John's status in the class. In fact, on a student questionnaire John indicated that he did not think it was important to address the issue of racism in class discussions. Other students who joked about race, such as Ron and James, did claim to have close friendships with students of color but actively resisted serious discussions of racism and denied the idea that racism still exists.

Joking about race served several functions for students at Excellence Academy. According to Radha and her friends, humor about race indicated a relaxed friendship and a desire to rise above the traditional restraints of racism. It is important to note, however, that Radha's group was composed of only white and Asian students and no African Americans. While I am not implying that Radha and her friends were racist because their friendship group did not include African Americans, I do think it is significant that they stayed within their comfort zone in their cross-racial friendships, that is, that whites in this group formed friendships only with members of the "model minority" (those who are stereotypically perceived to be higher achieving) and that Asian students in the group formed their closest friend-ships with whites (Shankar 2008; Wong et al. 1998). Joking about race allowed Radha and the "artsy nerds" to declare themselves nonracist with-out actually establishing and maintaining friendships with African Ameri-can students or even including them in small-group discussions assigned by Joann (as I describe later). Other students teased about race to elicit a response from their teacher, and possibly to make her feel uncomfortable. White students like John, Ron, and James resisted discussing racism in the classroom but freely joked about it during informal moments. Perhaps this combination of joking and resistance indicated that, ill equipped through inexperience to deal with the topic of structural racism and white privi-lege in contemporary society, students created their own spaces to address race. Joking about race allowed students to acknowledge the racial differ-ence that surrounded them in their daily school lives without examining the racial hierarchies that existed at school and in society. However, when Joann took the topic of race out of the realm of playing with difference and into discussions of inequity, power, and access, the joking was often replaced with anger on the part of white students.

Revisiting Students' Self-Segregation

In the midst of the relaxed, joking atmosphere at EA, as I describe in the previous chapter, students' racial self-segregation was prevalent. I revisit this practice here because, while self-segregation was not exclusionary, there were times that students' seating choices were nuanced by racial ten-sions. For example, when Joann asked Cathy, a white student, to move away from her white friends to a table where African American students were seated, Cathy refused, and, in Joann's words, "looked horrified." Joann then asked her, "Do you feel really strongly about this?" Cathy said, "Yes," and was allowed to remain with her white friends. Ryan, an African American female, was equally reluctant to join a group of white and Asian students for a class discussion, even though Joann had assigned her to that table. She sat quietly on the couch next to the table while the white and Asian stu-dents ignored her. I noticed Ryan's hesitancy to interact with the group and asked her if it was because she wasn't friends with the people at the table. "No, not that," she answered, "I just don't like to break into a group." Nev-ertheless, I had seen Ryan in this situation before and had noticed that she tended to quietly change her seat without Joann's permission in order to sit with African American or Latina students during group activities. Ryan and Cathy's experiences illustrate the "subtle exclusion" among students that Amanda Lewis (2006) describes, expressed in "a certain look" or "a certain tone of voice" (138). I'm not suggesting that it is unusual for adolescents to feel awkward with those not in their immediate friendship groups, but I am suggesting that in a school where "we all get along" is the party line, these incidents complicate that claim; at EA, "getting along" means the absence of overt racial conflict and does not necessarily suggest that racial divides and marginalization do not occur. And, while students may not have meant or even recognized these behaviors as marginalizing, there were times that their actions had that effect.

Noticing Marginalization

African American students noticed their marginalization in ways less routine than students' seating choices, illustrated by their response to school's handling of Black History Month. Every morning in homeroom during the month of February, a largely inaudible announcement was made, presumably honoring the achievement of African Americans in some way. We all chatted uninterrupted through these announcements until Joann reminded students to get quiet for the reciting of the school code of conduct and the Pledge of Allegiance that followed. Other than an assembly program that I describe shortly, these announcements were the only school-wide acknowledgment of Black History Month. Shallow attempts to recognize significant historical movements did not satisfy students at EA.

Excellence Academy's Code of Conduct
I am here to learn
Therefore I will

- Respect myself, others, and the environment.
- Cooperate with all school personnel.
- Do nothing to keep the teacher from teaching, or keep anyone, including myself, from learning.

The Negative Effect of Tokenism

Mary E. Thomas (2011) warns of the danger of tokenistic multicultural programming with purposes that "are unexplained and uncontextualized to students" (4). Such programming (sometimes referred to as uncritical multiculturalism) is problematic because it narrowly defines racial identity as cultural difference (McCarthy and Dimitriadis 2005; Nieto 2005; Sleeter 2005). Through token celebrations, students come to believe that racial equity is a matter of recognition, allowing them to remain uninformed of how past and present racial discrimination directly impacts their lives. Uncritical multiculturalism is likely to cause resentment in students of color (Thomas 2011); this, for many, was the case at EA, where African American students were aware that the school's attempt at multicultural recognition through the celebration of Black History Month was feeble at best.

An African American staff person at EA who had access to many classrooms over several years (and nervously asked that I not divulge any identifying information) told me that, as memory served, nothing concrete in the classroom had been done to help students explore their African American identity at school. Further, Joann's attempt to include more African American literature into her curriculum was not wholeheartedly supported by school administration; she'd had to argue to lengthen an eleventh grade unit on the Harlem Renaissance from three to nine days and feared her determination might result in a negative evaluation at the end of the school year. Although Joann was willing, lack of administrative support limited the amount of time students spent exploring Black History Month.

The one significant event offered to students in celebration of Black History Month was a late-day school assembly featuring a West African dance troupe, an interesting choice on the part of the administration since, other than the fact that the American slave trade derived its victims from West Africa, the program had nothing to do with American Black history. I entered the gym with the students that afternoon, sensing their excitement at the chance to get out of class for a while and do something fun. I was surprised to see that all three members of the dance troupe were white.[1] The vibrant drumbeats kept the students engaged and many danced at their seats. Then several African American and a few white students jumped up to join Joy, the main dancer, in a line at the front of the gym. The dancing continued through several numbers and then Joy introduced a "warrior song" that she said symbolizes "all those who choose to stand in solidarity with those who struggled in West Africa and in the civil rights movement." A characteristic of uncritical multiculturalism is its lack of accurate historical context; accordingly, Joy conflated events that were centuries apart with no explanation.

Joy then asked the students, "Y'all study Martin Luther King Jr., right?" A group of African American students sitting near the front shouted in unison and without hesitation, "No!" Joy looked surprised, but continued, "and Malcolm X, right?" Again, there was a loud "No!" from these students. Joann and I exchanged looks from the sidelines, surprised at the immediacy and cohesion of the students' reaction. It was as if these students knew Joy's questions were coming and had rehearsed their response, but of course they had not. The students' quick and unified response showed that they had noticed the absence of important African American historical figures in their curriculum. A social studies teacher was especially upset by the students' reaction to Joy's questions, claiming that, yes, they did "go over" Martin Luther King Jr. in her classes. While I don't doubt her word, from these African American students' perspective the time spent on African American history was inadequate.

In eleventh grader Lucky's view, EA was not the only school in the area that largely neglected the study of African American history. He told me in frustration that his old school, Carltonville High, a school with a black student population of 50 percent, "never" celebrated Black History Month. "But as soon as, like, Hispanic Heritage Month come around," he complained, "it's, like, parties, all that." Lucky's complaint illustrates Thomas's (2011) point that ethnic celebrations at schools can exacerbate racial tensions because of the vying for recognition these events cause among students. Like the girls that Thomas interviewed, Lucky expressed a "wounded otherness" (43) at his perceived exclusion and felt resentment toward another group, in this case Hispanics, who he believed got more attention from school administration. In reality, Thomas argues, no students benefit from the recognition these tokenistic celebrations bring because they divert attention from the reality of racial injustice that impacts their lives. Still, in the lived experience of students like Lucky, recognition was important, and the school administration's failure in this respect left them feeling slighted and resentful.

The Case of the Yellow Posters

During my interview with Lucky, he told me that he'd never experienced racism. However, when I asked if kids at school talked about race, he said the following:

LUCKY: Yes, about the school, like how the teachers, they think some of the teachers are racist.

MM: Oh really? Why do they think that? What kinds of things do teachers do that might make kids think that?

L: Like if a group of African Americans are talking, they would be like, "Be quiet and do your work." But soon as the Caucasian kids start talking, they be like, they won't even care. They just single every black person out in the class.

M: Hmm. And that happens pretty often, people feel like?

L: Yeah.

M: Has that, have you experienced that?

L: Yes.

The fact that, at first, Lucky did not recognize the favoring of white students over African Americans as a form of racism speaks to his own ambivalence about racism and perhaps to the ambivalent nature of race relations at the school. As friendly as the school was, Lucky indicated that the word was out among the black students: when it came to classroom disciplinary matters, they believed that white teachers favored white students. Although Lucky admitted that he had experienced this favoring system, he either did not immediately recognize it as racism or was not comfortable admitting that racism exists at the school. A bit later in the interview Lucky related other incidents of racism that he or his family had experienced: he had been followed around by store personnel as if he intended to steal merchandise, and when his sister and her white friend applied for the same retail position, the white friend received the job even though Lucky's sister had more work experience. Of the change in his position during our interview, Lucky explained, "I just had to think about it."

Lucky's responses show that he is in the process of figuring out what behaviors constitute racism and what impact these behaviors have on him personally. The ethos of racial harmony that exists at the school further complicates Lucky's process because to admit that white teachers favor white students challenges this ethos. It is also feasible that Lucky's initial response in which he minimizes the existence of racism in his personal experience reflects the colorblind approach that surrounds him; other researchers report similar responses from African American students. When probed more deeply, however, students identified ways that race did affect their everyday school lives (Lewis 2010; Winkler 2012).

Anthony described the dilemma African American students faced over their treatment by white teachers in a more nuanced way one day during a class discussion of *The Bluest Eye*. James, a white student, had insisted that "people are too sensitive" about race. Challenging dominant beliefs by using counternarrative (Kumasi 2011; Taylor 2009), Anthony responded with this story:

> Suppose a teacher singled out a certain group of kids for not doing their homework. I don't want to say what group—we'll just call them the—[glances up at yellow poster on wall]—"yellow posters." If all the yellow posters in the room get told, you didn't do your homework, even though some other kids, say, the "blue posters," didn't do their homework either, then they start to wonder, are we being singled out? But the truth is, they really didn't do their homework!

The discussion continued along these lines for several minutes, the class laughing every time Anthony used his poster analogy. He then told the story of how he had recently been stopped by the police while on the way to play basketball with his dad and a few friends. Since the gym was close to home and since he had no pockets in his gym attire, Anthony's father had left the house without his driver's license. A few blocks away from home they were stopped at a roadblock, where four police officers "jumped out of the cop car," ordered everyone out, handcuffed Anthony's father and pushed him against the car, and told Anthony to take his hands out of his pockets. Anthony's description of how the police found a bag of popcorn in the back seat and searched it for drugs provoked more laughter from the class.

Anthony used this example to illustrate that he and his father, like the "yellow posters," will never be sure of how much their race played a part in the events of that evening. The fact was that Anthony's father had no ID on him. Still, would they have received the same treatment by the police if they had been white? Anthony described quite adeptly the predicament that he and other people of color face regarding racial profiling—are they being singled out because of their race, or not? When Lucky was followed around by store employees, he assumed it was because he is black, but, he said, "maybe it's just ironic that I was being followed around" (I believe that Lucky meant to use the word "coincidental" here). Still, Lucky had noticed that store personnel had left whites of the same age alone. Pamela Perry (2008), a white college professor, relates the story of how a black college student accused her of racism when she inadvertently singled out the student for talking; a white student had been talking too, but Perry had not been able to remember the white student's name and so said nothing to her. A faulty memory may have been the cause of Perry's action, but from the African American student's perspective, race had been involved.

Derald Wing Sue and his colleagues (2007) refer to interactions such as those described by Lucky and Anthony as "racial microaggressions": "brief, everyday exchanges that send denigrating messages to people of color" (273). They describe the difficulty faced by people of color in determining if a microaggression has taken place, and the tendency to rely on patterns of past experience to make this determination. In the past, racism was more pronouncedly visible and easy to recognize (Bell 1992). Now that "bias is masked in unofficial practices," African Americans must "wrestle with the question whether race or some individual failing has cost us the job, denied us the promotion, or prompted our being rejected as tenants for an apartment" (Bell 1992, 6). Anthony's narratives were meant to illustrate the doubt that he and others experienced as possible targets of racism; while there may have been legitimate reasons for their negative interactions with whites, as in the case of the "yellow posters" at EA, it was impossible to know for sure if race had played a part.

Anthony laughed through the telling of his brush with the police, making the class laugh with him. When I suggested that, although we're laughing now, the incident probably wasn't funny when it happened, he largely brushed off that idea. A few minutes later, though, Anthony admitted to the class that he was angry that night, and that he and his dad "got the cops' badge numbers" but never followed through with a complaint. Even though he was angry about the incident, Anthony chose a comedic style for his narrative, perhaps because humor was the only tool at students' disposal to deal with the serious topic of racism without challenging the discourse of racial harmony at EA.

Juliette expressed a similar ambiguity when she referred to the lack of African American teachers at the school. She said, "I'm not saying it's intentional. It's not intentional, but it's odd, that's all. My mother said, 'Can't they find any African American teachers at that school?'" Through their responses, African American students expressed their difficult position: sometimes they felt sure about their marginalization, but at other times it was the not knowing, the uncertainty of racial favoring that added to the tensions they felt in this supposedly harmonious setting.

What's in a Word? Tensions over Language

Talking about race is often accompanied by hesitancy and confusion from students and teachers (Pollock 2004). White high school students may be uncomfortable talking about race partly due to unfamiliarity with racial terms (Lewis-Charp 2003). For example, some whites have trouble negotiating the terms *colored*, *black*, and *African American* (Trainor 2008). Racial tensions surfaced at EA over use of the term *black* as a racial descriptor during a tenth grade class group discussion of "A Class Divided," the *Frontline* (1985) documentary based on the famous "brown-eyed / blue-eyed" role-play exercise that third grade teacher Jane Elliott conducted with her students in 1968. The day after Dr. Martin Luther King Jr. was assassinated, Elliott explored the nature of discrimination with her white class by dividing them according to eye color and, on consecutive days, encouraging the ill treatment of one group by the other. I had asked the students what they thought of the video, knowing that it usually provokes strong emotional responses about the evils of racism. To my surprise, this was not the response I received that day. Instead, Ned, a white student, observed that if this exercise were done today, Elliott would be viewed as racist because of the language she used. Puzzled, I asked what he meant.

NED: Well, like, she uses the term *black*. If she said that now she'd be called racist.

MM: So just using the term *black* is racist? Like as opposed to "African American"?

N: I feel like it's seen that way. Like, if I pointed to someone across the street and said, "That black guy over there," that would be seen as racist.

M: Just for using the word to identity someone?

N: Yeah.

Hannah, an African American student, tried to help Ned understand how to use the term *black* appropriately. She explained: "It depends on how you say it. Like, if you just say, 'that black girl' [keeps voice light and even] it's not, but if you say, 'that *black* girl' [voice deepens, showing distaste on the word black], then it's racist." While many students did use the terms *black* and *African American* interchangeably (as has been my practice throughout this text), for others, like Ned, black was not a neutral term but was instead a racial slur. Hannah's explanation reinforced the idea that use of the term is risky business because if said in the wrong tone of voice, describing someone as "black" might leave one open to accusations of racism.

I followed up with Ned during an interview a few weeks later:

MM: There was one day when, um, we were talking at your table. And you guys were, some of the people at your table, mostly the guys, I guess, were saying that they were amazed at the fact that the teacher in the video used the terminology *black* . . .

NED: [interrupts] Yeah.

M: . . . so freely, because you felt that if she were to do that today, people would accuse her of racism.

N: Yeah. Um, that's a clear example of, um, someone modern-day just trying to call someone out for being racist, even if it's just saying the color of their skin. Like, uh, if an African American, if I went over and I called an African American "black," he would, stereotypically, he might come over and think I'm racist just because I called him black instead of African American. Same way for a black calling a white, like, "cracker" or something. If he came over and did that to him, he, the white, would think that he's being racist, 'cause he's calling him a derogative name.

M: Uh huh. So you think that the word black itself is a racial slur now, where it used to be just kind of a descriptive word?

N: I don't even want it to be a racist term. If you don't, I don't want to say [pause], all right, if, if you don't like being called a black, then you shouldn't be calling your other black friends "blackie" or that kind of stuff.

M: Has anybody ever, like, made it, has anyone ever made you feel like when you used that term, like, it offended them?

N: I try to stay away from saying anything like that.

M: So you haven't ever had that experience?

N: Yeah.

M: It's just kind of an idea that you've pick up just from kind of being around . . . people.

N: Yeah.

This conversation reveals much of what Ned thinks and feels about race. His use of the phrases, "if I went over," and "he might come over" indicate his awareness of the racial self-segregation that is prevalent at the school, since in his fictional scenario students are spatially segregated according to race. Once he travels "over" to talk, Ned envisions being accused of racism because he uses an improper racial descriptor. Although Ned has never actually had this experience, he has somehow internalized the fear of accusation. His statement, "I don't even want it to be a racist term" shows that he would have no racist intentions in using the word *black*, but it also reveals his discomfort over the situation. Thomas (2011) found that female students felt threatened and harassed by "stares" or "looks" from students of other backgrounds, but, the students admitted, "'you can't really prove it'" (103). She believes that the girls' fears are "indicative of the paranoid processes motivating girls' spatial practices at school" (104). In the same way, Ned shows a certain paranoia in the scenario he creates over use of the term *black*.

Perhaps it is inexperience that leads Ned, who told me that his neighborhood was "98 percent white," to equate the word *black* with *cracker*, a word that students clearly understood to be a racial slur toward whites. Admittedly, the number of racial descriptors available in English and the complex history of these words present a challenge for many people, youth and adults alike, who are unsure of how to use these terms correctly and inoffensively. However, as the conversation surrounding the *Frontline*'s "A Class Divided" continued that day, it became evident that some white students' hesitation in using the term "black" masked resentment over their perception that African Americans unfairly use their race to their advantage. During that class discussion, Bill, Ned's friend who is also white, stated his belief that racism is used as an excuse for "people" to get what they want. "Like," he said, "if you budge in front of someone on line and he says it's because of race when it isn't." Ned agreed, noting, "People just say someone is being racist toward them if they don't like what the person does, even though it has nothing to do with race." He explained, "That's why I don't think racism exists. People just use it as an excuse."

Bill confirmed this line of reasoning during our interview. I asked if he thought Elliott's use of the term *black* would lead to accusations of racism today.

BILL: Well, I think that it's just people trying to, like, contort society to get what they want.

MM: What people?

B: People that, that are not, that are not, again, not being, like, trying not to be racist here, but, that are not of what they think is the best class, of the best race, the best class of people. Um, and they're trying to use societal pressures on people to make them change. Um, like, I don't think, like, anyone, like, people, teachers use the word, like, for Aryan, they use the word, like, white. Which, that doesn't offend anybody. But all of a sudden you pull up the other color, other colors, like, uh, black, um, yellow, that, and all of a sudden, bam! You're off on a whole racist rant. Um, I think it's because that people who were treated unfairly back then feel like they need to get back at the people that were, that were mistreating them.

M: So you think that people of color . . .

B: Mmm

M: . . . are, um, kind of jump down people's throats for using those terms?

B: Yes.

M: And it's because they suffered so much in the past that now they think it's, like, their turn to be on top, or . . .

B: To be . . .

M: . . . to get back at . . .

B: to get back at society.

M: . . . at, at whites, basically?

B: Yes.

Much of what Bill said in this part of our interview indicates that he, like Ned, lacks the experience to use racial descriptors in context. For example, Bill's use of the term *Aryan* as a synonym for *white*, a term made famous by the Nazis and not widely used outside of extremist groups, is curious, but perhaps Bill's use of the word can be explained by the fact that he had recently heard it many times during the unit on Elie Wiesel's *Night* (1960). Additionally, Bill does not understand why the racial descriptor *white* is acceptable but the terms *black* and *yellow* are not. Here he not only mischaracterizes *black* as a racial slur but is unaware of the historical racism toward certain Asians groups that the term *yellow* connotes. It is also possible that, although the term *black* is not regarded as a racial slur and was used freely by other students at EA, Bill may have heard whites say the word in the same derogatory tone that Hannah described earlier.

Bill's comments reveal the tension that underlies his complaints over the use of racial descriptors. Bill believes that people of color—people who, he says, are "not of what they think is the best class, of the best race, the best class of people"—unfairly accuse whites of racism in order to "get what they want." It is not clear who "they" are in Bill's narration. Is Bill suggesting that "they," people of color, think poorly of themselves, or does Bill mean by this that society at large thinks poorly of people of color? Perhaps Bill uses this convoluted sentence construction to avoid specifically naming the group or groups to whom he refers, purposely distancing himself from racism (i.e., *they* think this, but *I* don't). In the same way, Bill's prefacing of this statement with the phrase, "trying not to be racist here" (a phrase he used several times during the interview), illustrates his fear of being falsely accused of racism but also signals that he knows what he is about to say could potentially be considered racist.

Other students in Bill and Ned's class showed they believed that merely talking about race opened one up to potential accusations of racism. Following is a class discussion that I recorded in my field notes during the unit on *Night*:

> As the students worked on their projects, Joann shared something her young daughter had asked last night: "Why is it that everybody is fine talking about sex and telling me everything I don't want to know about it, but nobody will talk about race?" Joann posed the question to the class.
>
> Ryan (African American female) responded quickly, "Because it's controversial." She thought for a second and then asked, "But why is it controversial?"

> FRAN (white female): Because people are afraid.
> MM: What are they afraid of?
> FRAN: Of being accused.
> MM: Being accused of what?
> NINA (white): Of being called racist.

As this segment indicates, students understood that, for many whites, racial identity is nuanced by anxiety over potential accusations of racism. For some, like Bill and Ned, this fear is accompanied by another commonly held discourse.

Whites as Victims

Just beneath the surface of Ned's and Bill's fears of racist accusation is the familiar discourse that positions whites as the new victims of racism. Bill's assessment of African Americans as people who are "trying to contort society to get what they want" and who act out of the "need to get back at . . . people" ignores the existence of racism in a present-day context. Moreover, Bill believes that blacks use accusations of racism to gain power over whites. Likewise, Ned's statement, "People just use it [racism] as an excuse," illustrates his belief that African Americans cry racism in order to gain benefits that they do not deserve. Bill and Ned responded in similar fashion as the white students at a different school who followed their musings over correct terminology ("colored," "African American," or "black") with the sentiments, "I think they think they're special," and "if you could get something for nothing, you'd do it. That's all they're doing" (Trainor 2008, 13). These students, like Ned and Bill, believe that whites are victimized on two levels. First, in order to protect themselves from unfair charges of racism, they are required to be especially careful about the language of race. No such requirement exists for African Americans, they believe, who are not only allowed to use the term *white* freely but can also, according to Ned, call each other "blackie" with impunity. Blacks are at a clear advantage here because they are allowed a freedom of expression not available to whites; therefore, a double standard exists. What's more, these students believe that this unfairness in language use exemplifies a deeper problem: African Americans may advance unfairly, placing themselves above whites in the racial hierarchy by accusing whites of racism. Although they "got along" with the African American students in their classes, for Ned and Bill, racial identity was infused with notions of unfairness and marginalization. Other white tenth graders expressed similar feelings of marginalization that eventually came to the surface in a heated classroom argument, described later in this chapter.

"Can I Just Call Them Black?"

Nakia, a black student who was born in the Virgin Islands, expressed some of the same sentiments and hesitations that Bill and Ned had shared. During our interview, she used the term *African American*, but then stopped and said, "do I have to call them that, or can I just call them black?" She went on in exasperation: "When, uh, like say, uh, a white person calls somebody, like, African American, it's like, I feel like they kind of go out their way. Just call, like, them black! Because that's what we're used to. Because, like, you don't hear us calling you guys Caucasian." Thus, Nakia introduces the word *Caucasian* into the mix, substituting it for *white* the way that Bill had done with *Aryan* and positioning it as the equivalent of *African American*.

A bit later in the interview Nakia stopped again midsentence, this time interrupting herself with a laugh. "Sorry," she explained, "I was thinking about a movie where, when, I think a white little guy, I can't remember the movie, but it was, like, a white little guy and he called, like, 'cause, you know how black people will be like, 'Oh, what's up my nigga' and stuff, and a white boy, like, went to a guy and was, like, 'Hi, what's up my nigga,' and, like, the guy was like, 'Oh my gosh, you're being racist' and like . . ." Again Nakia burst out laughing and didn't finish her sentence. I laughed too, partly because Nakia's laugh was infectious, but mostly because the naïve blunder of the "white guy" in the movie that she described was funny. Although Nakia had not been part of the conversation at Ned's table described earlier, the example from the movie that she found so humorous makes the very same point that Ned and Bill made: whites are held to a higher standard in adhering to racial language boundaries than blacks.

Nakia felt that both white and black people were oversensitive on the topic of race, saying of whites, "they make it awkward, like they're afraid to talk about it because of what happened in the past. And with slavery, and like Africans, and all of that." However, she held blacks more responsible for the problem than whites, as this interview segment shows:

MM: Ok, so it's, let me just go back to something you said, though. Because it, so that you can clarify, because it almost sounds like you're saying two different things. So on the one hand you're saying that black people are oversensitive about it, . . .

NAKIA: [laughs]

M: . . . right? And that they should kind of just get over it . . . 'cause slavery happened a long time ago.

N: Yeah, like, I'm not trying to say like, live and forget. It's like [pause] ok, like when slavery happened, it happened 'cause, like, they didn't think we were humans because we were black and stuff, and ok, I understand. That happened, and, but it's 2012, you can't hold a grudge for so long. You have to understand that what people did in the past, like, isn't what they're doing now. 'Cause they're not capturing us and making us, like, their slaves now. So, like, people have to understand it happened, and you have to understand it, and you have to, you can't live, like, hating white people for their past, because some white, like, the white people here, they weren't in the past, like, they, well, some of them, 'cause some people are still alive, like, they weren't in the past, they weren't doing that things, like, that happened, and like, we understand, it's wrong, and, it's, like [exasperated breath], I wanna tell 'em, like, but like they're holding a grudge for so long, and it's, it's not fair! . . . Like why hold a grudge for so long?

M: So, you think black people are oversensitive sometimes.

N: Yeah.

M: And you also think that white people are oversensitive sometimes.

N: Yeah, it's like, when it comes to race people are just very sensitive and, like, extra cautious about what they say . . . because they don't want to offend this person, or . . . that person, or feel offended [exasperated breath], like sometimes, like, people say the dumbest things, and they'll be like, oh, that was racist, and like, and, it's like people are so quick to judge someone and be like, oh, you were racist, like 'cause you're white, and you said that thing. But if a black person says it, it's like, oh, you're fine.

Nakia starts out by saying that both black and white people are at fault in being "oversensitive." She is exasperated at both groups, wishing for both to "get over" their anxiety about race. However, she soon shifts her narrative to show sympathy for whites. Like Ned and Bill, she believes that blacks are unfairly allowed more leeway in their use of racial language than whites ("But if a black person says it, it's like, oh, you're fine"). Not stopping there, she aligns herself with the position that African Americans use past racism to try to advance unfairly in the present when she states: "But, I feel like, sometimes, like, [laughs] African Americans, I feel like they get upset, and they get sensitive about it because of what happened, like slavery, and yes, we understand that it was wrong, but they like, they feel like people owe them things and stuff." Here, Nakia separates her experience from that of African Americans by using the pronoun "they." Perhaps because she spoke so quickly or perhaps because she couldn't quite decide if she identified herself with African Americans, blacks, or neither, throughout the interview Nakia switched back and forth from first-person to third-person pronouns.

Nakia identified her best friend as Kiya, one of the white girls who was directly involved in the argument over race in the tenth grade on-level class that I discuss shortly. My interview with Nakia took place a little over a week after that event. Although Nakia was in a different class and was not involved in the argument, it is likely that she heard a full rendition of the event from Kiya's perspective. Much of what she said during our interview was similar to the sentiments her friend expressed on the day of the argument and during my interview with her, and to the arguments of her own white classmates and other white students: blacks ("they") use cries of past racism (slavery) to gain present, unearned benefits (Trainor 2008). The fact that Nakia hails originally from St. Thomas may also be a factor in her pronoun switching and in her alignment with white students in issues of race and racism (Waters 2001).

In spite of her depiction of African Americans as people who believed "people owed them things," as our interview continued Nakia related two incidents when she had personally felt the effects of racism. Once, she explained, store personnel had ignored her but had greeted her white friend (who had entered the store a few minutes later) warmly, and a second time, during a golf tournament, white spectators had ignored her but had cheered the white golfers enthusiastically. In that context she clearly understood racism as a present-day phenomenon that she herself had experienced. In retrospect, I wondered if Nakia's statements about African Americans holding grudges and feeling owed something because of long-past racism reflected her attempts to view racism from the perspective of her white friend, Kiya. It seemed that Nakia struggled to reconcile the need to construct her white best friend as not-racist with her own experiences as a target of racism at the hands of whites.

Thus far, this chapter has shown that both African American and white students felt racially marginalized in this racially harmonious school. While some black students felt that their heritage was ignored or believed that they were singled out for disciplinary issues by white teachers, some white students felt marginalized through too-quick judgments on the part of blacks that led to false accusations of racism.

Tensions for Teachers

Students were not the only stakeholders at the school who experienced tensions over race; teachers, too, felt anxieties over race that impacted their pedagogical decisions. One white teacher, Lisa, went to great lengths to adjust her teaching methodology because of that anxiety.

The Language of Snowflakes

It would be easy to brush off Ned's claim that African Americans cry racism "if they don't like what the person does" as an example of a white youth's refusal to acknowledge racism. However, Mica Pollock (2004) found that, at times, students of color behaved exactly as Ned described. Sensing teachers' discomfort in talking about race, students occasionally used accusations of racism to get back at teachers with whom they'd had problems. Lisa, who had been teaching at EA for several years, described a similar incident to me during our interview. She had told a class of mostly African American students (many of them the same students that had responded with a loud "No!" to Joy's questions during the African dance program) that they were "all unique snowflakes." This was not the first time Lisa had used this metaphor with students; she and other teachers often compare students to snowflakes in an effort to encourage students to appreciate their individual strengths. She was surprised and dismayed, however, when her African American students "took exception to snowflakes, and told me black ice would be more appropriate than snowflakes." Of course, Lisa did not mean her comment to refer to race in any way. She did not mention the whiteness of snowflakes, only their uniqueness. Did these students really believe that Lisa's words were racially insensitive? I don't think so. But by implying that Lisa had referred to race with her snowflake illustration, these African American students fashioned racial language from a heretofore nonracial term, an action that served them on two levels. First, the students' teasing comments again signify the use of humor as a release for feelings of marginalization that bubbled under the surface of the school's friendly environment. Second, by taking the opportunity to make Lisa squirm a little with the mischievous implication that her illustration was racist, African American students appropriated the power of their white teacher and temporarily shifted the usual white–black, teacher–student power balance in their classroom. They coped with the marginalization they felt at school by marginalizing a white teacher in that moment in time as a possible racist. Interestingly, as we see below, Lisa responded to accusations of racism by covering up the function of race in academic achievement with these very same students. Hence, racial tension moved from students to teacher to students in a cyclical pattern of "getting along" at Excellence Academy.

Avoiding the "Racially Charged"

Although it is likely that Lisa's students were teasing her during the snowflake episode, for Lisa the incident was anything but funny. Past accusations from students and their parents had caused serious difficulties for teachers at EA. Previously that school year one such circumstance had arisen; an African American male student had accused a white female teacher of racism, apparently because of something she had said as a joke. Of course, no one was supposed to know about this highly confidential situation, but of course everyone did. It was understandable, then, that uneasy classroom moments over race fostered teachers' fears of accusation and that these fears affected teachers' relationships with students and their pedagogical choices. The following account illustrates how Lisa tailored her pedagogy based on these fears.

One day, during Joann's prep period, Lisa burst into the room brimming with enthusiasm. She had recently attended a teachers' conference and was thrilled at the success she'd had implementing one of the techniques she had learned with her students. Instead of uniformly giving students the same classwork, homework, quizzes, and final assessment, she had applied a technique in differentiating instruction that had really seemed to work for her students. She had quizzed students at the beginning of the unit and separated them into groups based on their scores, working longer with students who needed help early in the unit and not allowing any students to move ahead until they had shown mastery of the subject. She had also stopped giving credit for effort alone so that students could not "squeak by," passing the marking period without actually passing assessments. Lisa was thrilled with the results, reporting that all students had received a passing grade for the unit.

In order to determine which students needed extra work, Lisa had to designate a cut-off in the students' initial quiz scores. The original passing grade was 65 percent, but Lisa had noticed that all of the students who scored below that grade were African American. Lisa was "nervous" about this, so (without telling the students) she moved the passing grade to 70 percent, so that a white student would be included in the group that failed the quiz. During an interview a few days later I pressed Lisa on this choice. She justified the decision to raise the passing grade for the quiz by saying that the white student now included in the failing group would benefit from the extra help. "There really was no downside to that," she explained. Lisa worried about her decision, though, saying, "I'm not used to finding myself making decisions based on considerations of race." She explained:

LISA: I was concerned if I stuck with the 65 percent or below all African American population that someone might, that, that a student might perceive that as racist . . . or [pause], if not racist, racially charged in some way. And I want, I was interested in defusing that. I felt that I was, I knew, without a doubt that I wasn't being racist, I was confident the administration wouldn't think I was being racist, but I didn't want any irrational justification for not, for this activity not being successful.

MM: Right. So . . . on one hand, you wanted to have diversity in that group so that a student wouldn't look at it and misunderstand.

L: Yes.

M: But on the other hand . . . did you, like, fear that by changing your criteria because you wanted diversity that you might open yourself up, not that you thought it would really happen, but the thought was there that . . .

L: [interrupts] Yeah! Like wow! I'm having to think about this.

M: . . . you might be critiqued in another, in the opposite way.

L: By fellow professionals in another way. Yeah!

M: Right, right. So in a way . . .

L: Yes! [laughs]

M: . . . you're kind of in between, and whatever you do . . . isn't right. Or, there's a fear that it might be perceived . . .

L: That, that there are definitely outsiders looking in who would take exception to either course of action.

M: Right. So you're kind of in a, in a difficult situation.

L: Right. Yes.

Although she felt sure that in her decision to change the grading scale for her class she was not being racist, Lisa worried that the appearance of a group of failing students composed exclusively of African Americans would be "racially charged" in some way. This term, one that I had heard other teachers use, is softer than the word *racist*, but I believe that in this context Lisa meant she feared being accused of racism. While Lisa didn't think anyone could actually make this case against her, she worried that what she meant as a technique to help students succeed academically would become complicated by the topic of race. "I wanted to take the course of action that was going to lead the activity to be as successful as possible," she explained. During our interview Lisa realized she was in a no-win situation; had she done nothing, the black students might accuse her of racism, but by altering the cut-off score, she had opened herself up to accusations of racism on a different level. She had violated the unspoken colorblind code that insists that academic achievement stand apart from racial considerations. By considering race in a grading practice, Lisa had broken a strong taboo. The strength of colorblind rhetoric among preservice and in-service teachers helps explain Lisa's anxiety about her actions (Choi 2008).

One might also argue that Lisa's choice, if found out, could lead to accusations of reverse racism, since, after all, the white student had not really failed the quiz. Her epiphany during our interview ("Yeah! Like wow! I'm having to think about this") shows that she had not fully realized the untenable nature of her position during her decision-making process. No matter what course of action Lisa took, the accusation of racism might follow.

More importantly, Lisa's anxiety and interest in "defusing" any possibility of a "racially charged" response stood in the way of her asking some fundamental questions: why is it that the African American students in her class were the lowest achievers? What societal systems worked to create this situation, and how can educators work to correct those systems? Instead, Lisa uncharacteristically considered race in order to create the appearance that race played no part in the achievement demographics of her class. Lisa's behavior confirms Pollock's (2004) argument that teachers do notice race but choose to be "colormute" for fear of uncomfortable repercussions. As Pollock points out, failure to talk about race ultimately makes race matter more, not less, as important questions regarding inequitable systems remain unaddressed.

Joann confessed to me on many occasions that she, like Lisa, felt anxious when talking about race with her students. She, too, feared accusations of racism but also of "losing control" during class discussions, a fear perhaps born from Joann's intuitive perception of the tensions brewing beneath the surface of her usually calm classes. To combat the threat of potential accusations, Joann used narrative to position herself as "not racist" during class discussions and in her conversations with me. For example, one day during the tenth grade unit on *Night*, Jada begged Joann to "tell that story about the skinheads again." Joann complied and told of how many years ago, when she was in high school, skinheads had attacked her. Joann did not explain what these individuals had against her, which furthered the impression that it was her very nonracist nature they objected to. She described how these ruffians had caught up with her in a deserted area of the school with intent to do serious harm. They had encircled her, brass knuckles in hand, and the situation was so dire that right before they struck, Joann told us, "I came to peace with my death." Then, in the nick of time, a friend from the basketball team saw what was about to take place through the crack of a closing door and led the entire team to Joann's rescue, taking down the skinheads in a brawl that left Joann shaken but unharmed. While Joann used colorblind ideology in that she did not mention the race of her rescuers (or of her attackers, for that matter), their identification as members of the basketball team at Joann's racially mixed high school implied that they, or at least some of them, were African American. Through this story Joann positioned herself firmly against a white racist group and on the side of African Americans, who helped her because of her friendship with them. Mary Bucholtz (2011) notes that students created a hierarchy of racialized masculinity through employing the trope of the physically powerful black male; in Joann's version of this theme, her rescuers were powerful enough to defeat a group of whites bearing weapons. While I don't doubt the veracity of Joann's story, I find her tendency to use storytelling to position herself as a friend of African Americans and an enemy of racist whites to be a significant indication of the anxiety she felt over how students would perceive her as a white person.

Tensions Rise to the Surface

Because of her commitment to social justice, Joann tried to push past her anxieties on the subject of race, intentionally including texts in her curriculum that explored themes of oppression and bringing up racism in class discussions during the teaching of these texts. One such text was Ishmael Beah's 2007 memoir *A Long Way Gone*, the compelling story of Beah's brutal experiences as a child soldier during the civil war in Sierra Leone in the 1990s. Coincidentally, the tenth grade reading of Beah's text coincided with the viral release of Invisible Children's emotionally laden KONY 2012 video. The video described the atrocities of Joseph Kony, a rebel leader in northern Uganda accused of recruiting child soldiers into his Lord's Resistance Army. As a result, much class time during this unit was spent debating the claims of the video. Students also explored Beah's references to the loss of his childhood innocence, a major theme in the book, and discussed whether or not he and others like him should have been held legally accountable for their actions. They held varying strong opinions on these topics, leading to lively and engaged class discussions. On the surface, all seemed well until the day that racial tensions unexpectedly erupted into a heated exchange that left Joann and the students rattled.

The Spectrograph Game

I had been away at a conference for a few days and returned to my hotel room one evening to find a panicked e-mail from Joann asking that I call her immediately. Her voice shaking, Joann described in detail what had transpired in the tenth grade on-level class that day. The dialog in the following account is recreated based on the rendition of the events that Joann related to me that evening and reiterated in a subsequent interview.

Joann had been leading an activity called "The Spectrograph Game" that had spiraled out of control. Following the directions in a publisher's curriculum guide, Joann had run a strip of masking tape down the center of the room to divide it into two sections. She then read a series of statements and asked the students to move to one side of the tape or the other depending on whether they agreed or disagreed with the statement; the more strongly they agreed or disagreed, the further from the tape on opposite sides of the room they were told to stand. All was well until Joann read the following statement: "The message of this book [Beah's memoir] would be different if it were written about a white man and set in a predominantly white country." In response, the white students moved to the far edge of the "disagree" side of the room, while the African American students moved to the far edge of the "agree" side. Three African American females, Jada, Dawn, and Adana, adamantly agreed with the statement, Jada claiming that "It wouldn't change the message, but it wouldn't have gone on so long. Nobody cares when stuff like this happens to black people." The girls contended that the rest of the world would have intervened, stopping the war and rescuing child soldiers if the events in Beah's life had happened to a white person in a predominately white country. Dawn argued, "White people's problems are everybody's problems, but black people's problems are only black people's problems." Joann reported that Becca and Bubbles, both white and both friendly with African American students in the class, disagreed from the other side of the room, insisting, "It isn't about race."

Up until this point the discussion had been civil, but when Brit and Kiya, also white, got involved, emotions began to intensify. They, too, stood far from the tape on the "disagree" side of the room, insisting, "It's not fair, because black people are just as racist toward white people." As evidence, they both said that they had personally been "harassed" by black people. Kiya complained in anger, "I'm sick of being accused of being racist. Every time a white person says anything about race they get accused of being racist. That's racist against white people. Black people are racist too!"

Dawn countered, "You have no idea how much easier you have it as a white girl. You have no idea how hard it is to be a black girl in this country." Jada agreed and said, "Racism will never change, because white people won't talk about it, so nothing will ever change." During this discussion, which purportedly was becoming more heated with every passing moment, the African American males in the class said nothing but sat near the African American girls with their arms folded. The racial segregation of the room was a physical representation of the deep division of these students' opinions.

Tom, a white male, tried to be, in Joann's words, "a unifying agent." He agreed with Jada, Dawn, and Adana but also shared that during the 2008 presidential election he was afraid to express his conservative political views because as "soon as I said something against Obama I was accused of racism." While everyone agreed with Tom that his scenario was accurate and that his treatment was unfair, by now the argument had gone too far and none of the girls were willing to back down. Joann reported that they got louder and louder, accusing each other of rudeness and yelling over each other until she had to stop the activity. All of this took place within the last ten minutes of class time and happened so quickly that the argument got out of control before Joann could intervene. Joann estimated that it took her about twenty seconds to get the girls to stop shouting at each other. "That doesn't seem long," she said, "but it's a long time to not have control of a class." She finally had to position herself between the arguing girls in order to "break eye contact" so that they would stop shouting. Although Joann tried to defuse the situation by telling students that the classroom needed to be a "safe space" for these kinds of conversations, students left class angry and frustrated, with no sense of resolution or closure.

Dealing with the Aftermath

Joann was close to tears as she told me about this incident. She said in frustration that while she now understood the social constructionist view of race, "I still hate the idea of races. We should all be just the human race." It was evident that the students, too, were frustrated by the incident. The next day the students wanted to continue their debate, but Joann refused to let them. She felt they needed time to calm down and asked them to write about their feelings instead in the form of a "racism survey," a brief questionnaire she constructed that asked of their experiences and feelings about racism. In response to the questionnaire prompt "When discussing racism in the classroom, what rules do you think should be in place?" every student made reference to their discomfort surrounding the events of the day before with statements like, "Don't raise your voice," "Don't speak over each other," and "Calmly talk about the topic." Joann hoped that the class could continue the discussion on the following Monday, when I would be back at school to support her in mediating students' responses. However, by then the students were back to their usual friendly demeanor, and if Joann had not told me what had happened I would never have known of the serious dispute that had taken place just a few days before. During class Joann showed a PowerPoint presentation that described modern-day forms of structural racism and included a map that indicated the presence of currently existing hate groups. Although the students listened politely and with moderate interest, the conversation remained calm and impersonal. The intensity of emotion had faded, and students once again discussed racism as something that existed in the outside world but did not impact them directly.

Students' Perspectives

As I prepared to interview students from this class in the coming weeks, I worried about how I might broach the subject of the argument. I feared they had been so upset during the incident that they might not want to discuss their feelings with me, an outsider. I need not have worried; Jada, one of the African American girls in the class, and Brit and Kiya, both white, were eager to talk about what had happened. Jada actually brought up the topic before I did, and Brit and Kiya, who I interviewed together, sat up straight and said, "Yeah, oh yeah!" when I asked if they were okay with talking about the argument that had transpired in their class.

During our interviews, all three girls reiterated the positions they had taken in class. Jada said, "I just think that African Americans or black people or people of a different color have, have it harder, because people still think that they're superior over [pause] us." When I asked Jada why she thought there had been so much anger from students that day, she said, "I think they felt attacked. But, I don't think they were. I don't, I didn't really understand why they felt attacked, 'cause, I remember one girl said that what we were saying was rude. And I didn't quite understand how she thought what we were saying was rude when it was about us." However, while holding her position firmly, Jada was careful to clarify her feelings about the white members of the class: "I think they were thinking that we were just saying, [deepens voice] 'Oh, all white people are just mean and ignorant and that you guys did this,' but I mean, it's not you guys, it's just people who have this instinctular, who think differently than you. We're not saying, grouping you all together, it's just people who have different ways of thinking."

Jada stressed that she was not accusing her classmates of racism; neither does she believe that all white people are racist. About her own feelings that day, Jada did not admit anger. She stated, "I had no bad feelings with anybody. . . . I think people thought I was mad 'cause I was kind of yelling. But I was just trying to get my point across." This is a very different story than the one Joann had told; she had specifically pointed out to me how horrible she felt about the events of that day because of "the look on Jada's face" at the end of class. According to Joann, Jada had been devastated by the incident. Since I had heard about Jada's reactions on the day of the argument through Joann's lens, it is impossible for me to know the extent of Jada's anger that day. However, by Jada's own admission, the people around her during the debate believed that she was angry and upset. But by the time of our interview several weeks later, the anger Jada expressed over the marginalization of African Americans was once again safely out of view.

Brit and Kiya, too, repeated the sentiments they had expressed in class during our interview, insisting that all groups were equally racist toward one another. Kiya said:

There's not one race that's singled out that gets the most white people racist toward them. I mean, they were saying that, like, black people always are, like, targeted, and not white people and stuff, but I'm like, well if I were to move into a community, like, that was all black, and, like, to a school and everything, I was, like, one of the few white kids, I would guarantee that I would get made fun of, picked on, same with if it was the other way around.

Brit agreed, saying:

Racism is everywhere, and no person can say they haven't been racist once in their life, whether it be a thought or you saying it. Like, it's not just one race that we're racist against. Black people are racist against white. White are racist against black. Mexicans, Chinese—it's everywhere. And just for one race to say that they're targeted, yes, they were, like over hundreds and hundreds of years ago, but it's not like we're still doing that now. We're actually working on it.

Through their belief that "racism is everywhere" and that whites are equally targeted, Kiya and Brit avoided admitting that, as their African American classmates pointed out, as white girls, they hold a position of privilege.

Kiya and Brit were quick to admit that there was racism at their school, but both felt it was mostly blacks that were racist toward whites. Their feelings were consistent with those of other white students who, when asked to define racism, could only think of examples of racism against whites (Marx 2006). And, while Jada was clear that she was not accusing her classmates or whites in general of racism, Brit and Kiya stressed that they had been falsely accused of racism and that blacks were oversensitive about the subject. They aired the same sentiment that their friend Nakia had expressed: black people need to stop "holding a grudge" for the racist actions of the past (Beach, Thein, and Parks 2008).

Kiya, Brit, and Jada all mentioned Joann's follow-up PowerPoint presentation about modern examples of structural racism, but with very different opinions. Jada believed that Joann's lesson had been helpful in clarifying her position, saying about it, "I think it kind of changed people's minds, somehow." I'm not sure which people Jada was referring to, but during my interview with Brit and Kiya it became clear that their minds had not been changed. Rather, they had felt marginalized by Joann's presentation, saying that Joann had "dominated the black side more than the white side." (In fact, I noticed that although some of the hate groups listed on the map

Joann showed were black separatist groups, Joann did not point this out and class discussion proceeded on the assumption that all of the highlighted groups were white supremacists.) Brit and Kiya were not alone in their perception: during a unit on white privilege, white students at a different school also felt that teachers cut them off and "'sided with students of color more'" (Flynn 2012, 107).

Given that schools in the United States are immersed in a dominant neoliberal ideology that stresses equal opportunity and meritocracy and attributes failure to a lack of a strong work ethic or other negative cultural characteristics (Ochoa and Pineda 2008), it is not surprising that students like Kiya and Brit would view racism as primarily a problem among individuals and not as a systemic, structural social problem. Neoliberalism, a way of thinking that has dominated social and economic philosophy and influenced racial discourse for decades (May and Sleeter 2010), insists that governments stay out of economics and allow the free market to determine what businesses and services flourish through raw competition (Penn 2008). By giving primacy to the unregulated market, neoliberalism promotes privatization of formerly public services like education under the assertion of "choice." Charter schools like Excellence Academy owe their very existence to neoliberalism since it was the growing influence of the free market approach that led to the passing of charter school legislation in the 1990s that allowed the privatization of public schools.

Neoliberal discourses mask racial inequity by stressing the modern workings of fairness and equal opportunity (Choi 2008) and insisting that race is no longer a significant social force (Giroux 2008). Posing as race neutral, such arguments serve the interests of whites through their emphasis on choice and individuality and de-emphasis on the systemic forms of racism that have long upheld white advantage (Salter and Adams 2013). Hence, neoliberal thinking has successfully privatized racial discourse by limiting the definition of racism to acts of individual prejudice (Giroux 2008). Having grown up hearing and believing that racism is a diminishing problem practiced by a few small-minded people and that anyone can achieve greatness if he or she works hard enough, it is understandable that students like Kiya, Brit, and others would deny claims of institutional racism toward African Americans and would view attempts to rectify the effects of racist systems as the unfair favoring of black over whites.

Toward the end of our interview Kiya admitted the existence of structural racism by saying "a lot of them in the hood don't have good education," However, she took a defensive position about the facts Joann had presented during the PowerPoint lesson, explaining, "it's, like, not our fault, you know. It's kind of the way they were brought up, just like we're brought up." With this statement, Kiya shifted the onus away from the racist structures inherent in our inequitable educational system and toward people's individual failings (presumably parents and family: "It's kind of the way they were brought up"). Further, although Joann was careful to state several times throughout her lesson that "it's not the fault of anyone in this room," Kiya still felt the need to absolve herself of blame ("it's, like, not our fault"). Regardless of Joann's attempts to assure students otherwise, white students like Kiya felt threatened or judged when the topic of racism was discussed (Flynn 2012).

Although the racial tensions I describe in this chapter represent a power struggle among students and teachers, we must also consider the particular powerlessness and frustration that working-class white students speak from when they voice their opinions about race. Scholars have noted that white students from lower economic backgrounds feel marginalized because they resent both the more affluent whites whose parents have the ability to support them through college and the students of color who might benefit from scholarships not available to whites (Beach, Thein, and Parks 2008). For this reason, many white students at EA had difficulty seeing themselves as privileged or as the beneficiaries of racism. Many of them from lower economic areas in and around Carltonville rode buses with African American students. They felt they were not privileged and not overtly racist but rather were friendly toward others of differing racial backgrounds. As such, they did not understand Joann's and my claims that racism is still an issue or that whites hold an advantaged position in society. Broad conversations about institutional racism made them feel as if they were being blamed for something that they'd had nothing to do with, and they responded defensively during class discussion about race.

Mexicans and Muslims

Interestingly, students at EA did not completely deny the existence of racism, only its focus. Along with declaring whites as the new victims of racism, many students, Kiya and Brit included, mentioned Mexicans and Muslims as targeted groups. However, white and black students referred to these groups to bolster different arguments. Black students acknowledged racism against their own group but pointed out that blacks can be racist toward Mexicans and Muslims. White students cited Mexicans and Muslims as targets of racism to prove their point that racism has decreased against African Americans; that is, blacks are not the only group that experience racism—Mexicans and Muslims experience it even more than blacks. Application of Bell's (2009) interest convergence theory may shed light on white students' willingness to admit racism toward some groups (Mexicans and Muslims) and not others (African Americans). Interest convergence, a key element of critical race theory, claims that whites will only speak for racial equality when it advances their own interests; they will not support policies that threaten their status of dominance. While it is important for all students to look past the black/white binary in their discussions of racism (Flynn 2012), it is also true that there were no Mexicans or Muslims in any of Joann's literature classes, and if there were any at the school, they were very few in number. Therefore, admitting racism toward these groups and showing concern for them did not threaten the status of the white students at EA. White students could adopt antiracist positioning toward Mexicans and Muslims because such positioning was in their interests: through their concern for these groups they elevated themselves to the politically correct not-racist status. Conveniently, the lack of students at the school from either of these backgrounds ensured that white students were in no danger of losing their socially dominant status to them. However, admitting the damaging and persisting effects of structural racism on African Americans would be tantamount to acknowledging white privilege, clearly not something Kiya, Brit, and other white students were prepared to do.

Moving On or Pushing Down?

While Brit and Kiya maintained a friendly demeanor in class during the days and weeks following the argument over race, their animated responses during our interview made clear that the racial tensions they expressed that day in class were still very much on their minds. However, by the following Monday after the argument took place, Joann said she felt the students had "moved on." Shrugging her shoulders, she said, "They're like little kids. They have a fight one day and are back to being best friends the next." She did not recognize the possibility that, rather than having moved on, the students had once again suppressed the racial tensions that existed among them. By not allowing the students to continue their discussion the day after the argument, Joann had unknowingly sent a clear message that she was not comfortable with what had taken place and that feelings about racism were best handled through the impersonal media of a questionnaire and PowerPoint presentation. In retrospect, I realize that I was complicit in sending this message, agreeing with Joann that it might be better to give the students time to cool off before continuing the discussion. Instead of challenging students to think deeply about the disagreements that had arisen among them, focus on students' emotional comfort became our priority (Haviland 2008). The problem with this strategy was that, while Joann continued to address the topic of institutional racism in her class, she never addressed the raw emotion the students displayed over the subject. Tom pointed out in his questionnaire that conversations about racism "may actually bring heightened tensions," and I believe that was the case for the tenth graders at EA. Rather than helping students to understand and empathize with others' points of view, the argument over race precipitated by discussion of *A Long Way Gone* exacerbated racial tensions and left students with the uneasy confirmation that it is dangerous to talk about race.

The Myth of the Safe Space

Joann's intention was to use multicultural literature to open a space for conversation about the important topic of racism. She hoped that discussion of *A Long Way Gone* would encourage students to consider multiple perspectives and develop ideas about race that would incorporate antiracist understandings. Coupled with her own caring and supportive presence, Joann imagined this space would be a safe one—a place where students could share their feelings freely without fear of ridicule or rejection, and she stressed this to her students as she tried to calm their flaring tempers. However, students' racial identities consisted of a complex blend of racial tolerance (illustrated by the close friendships between students and the usually relaxed atmosphere) and resentments over perceived racial marginalization. White teachers, whose professional life depended on their "not-racist" personas, felt deep anxiety over possible accusations of racism that characterized their identity as whites.

Therefore, classrooms at EA were not safe spaces for students when it came to discussing personal experiences and ideas about race; nor were classrooms safe spaces for teachers. Instead, classrooms were places where black students noticed when white teachers ignored their history and wondered if they were singled out for reprimand because of the color of their skin. Classrooms were places where white students and teachers feared accusations of racism. They were places where students believed that blacks cried racism as a ploy to get what they wanted. For one tenth grade class, the classroom was a place where literature functioned as a conduit but not one through which they might see the world in a more enlightened way (Botelho and Rudman 2009). Instead, for these students literature acted as a conduit through which bottled up tensions escaped and exploded when they hit the unrelenting surface of other people's experiences.

While Joann's intentions in proclaiming her classroom a "safe space" for discussions of race were noble, in retrospect I believe that too much emphasis on emotional safety while discussing race may do more harm than good. For example, was it Nakia's desire to keep her white friends emotionally safe that led her to argue that blacks unfairly hold grudges about slavery, even though she herself had experienced racism in a present-day, localized context? Was it the desire to return to the safety of a "friendly" classroom atmosphere that prevented Joann from helping tenth graders to debrief about their argument? Many researchers have found that race is not often spoken about in school settings (Beach, Thein, and Parks 2008; Lewis 2006; Marx 2006; McIntyre 1997); perhaps the desire for emotional safety over the topic of racism is part of the reason for this silence. The truth is that race is not a safe topic because it brings up deep-seated emotions, fears, and anxieties that are the product of centuries of broken race relations. Of course, no student should feel singled out because of race, and teachers should discuss the effects of racism on all people (Perry 2008). Certainly, teachers need to require a respectful environment in which all voices are heard when talking about race or any other subject (Chadwick 2008). However, a respectful environment is not the same as a so-called safe environment; talking about race is often emotionally risky for both students and teachers, and we should acknowledge that fact from the outset and prepare students for the tensions that will inevitably result from their sharing of differing perspectives (Beach, Thein, and Parks 2008; Flynn 2012).

Teachers like Joann need support and training in order to manage discussions of racism and other challenging social issues. Those teachers who are overly concerned with emotional safety in class discussions may fail to adequately support and challenge students as they grapple with difficult issues that have no easy answers. Expectations that students will feel comfortable in talking about race may be inappropriate; Elizabeth de Freitas and Alexander McAuley (2008) argue that the final goal of racial identity development for whites should not be comfort but discomfort, and that whites should experience a sense of continuing ambiguity that "resists the comfort of closure" (433) regarding their privilege and dominance. Forming opinions about topics such as racism should be a process that takes place over a period of time, and it is more important to help students "accept ambiguity and recognize the limitations of their own perspectives" (Beach, Thein, and Parks 2008, 220) than to expect them to process complicated issues simplistically and safely. Adopting such an approach might help students and teachers at EA to address the feelings of marginalization, resentment, and anxiety that surrounded the topic of race and might prevent these feelings from festering beneath the surface of "we all get along."

3

Discourse among Friends

■ ■ ■ ■ ■ ■ ■ ■ ■ ■ ■ ■ ■ ■ ■ ■ ■

The Harlem Renaissance Unit

As we saw in the last chapter, the friendly, relaxed atmosphere at Excellence Academy did not represent the whole story of race relations at the school, and may have made underlying tensions easier to ignore. Feelings of marginalization complicated students' racial identities, in one case erupting into an argument that the teacher could barely contain. Students in other classes, as well, responded to multicultural literature in ways that revealed the complexity of their constructions of race and their racial identities. In this and the next chapter I investigate eleventh grade honors students' responses to two literature units: the poetry of Langston Hughes during a unit on the Harlem Renaissance, and *The Bluest Eye*, by Toni Morrison.

The eleventh grade honors class stood out for its outspoken and consistent claims of close-knit, cross-racial friendships among students. Early on in my fieldwork, Joann described these friendships to me. Many, she told me, had "been together since kindergarten," a situation that, in her view, sometimes made staying on track during class discussions challenging because students were so comfortable with each other. During interviews students in this class confirmed what I had heard from Joann, as did students' demeanor and body language during class sessions. It was common for students to squeeze together on the couch at the back of the room, sometimes whispering or laughing, and other times simply sitting quietly, comfortable in each others' presence. I also saw students exchange hugs or backrubs and share snacks on a fairly frequent basis, and these behaviors often crossed racial boundaries. Until conversations about race became particularly uncomfortable toward the end of the school year, racially self-segregated seating arrangements were less common in this class than in others, and at the beginning of my field-work Violet and Juliette (both African American) often sat with James and Ron (both white) and referred to their group as "family."

However, in the midst of these close cross-racial friendships, students voiced frustration, resentment, and anger during discussions of literature that incorporated the theme of racial oppression. And while there was no single blowout argument among students in 11 Honors, resentment and frustration leaked slowly and steadily from them throughout the literature units that explored the topic of race. This chapter shows how white students created specific, contextualized discourses to avoid acknowledging racism as they studied the works of Langston Hughes.

Discussing the Poems of Langston Hughes

Although she had to push hard for administrative approval, Joann suc-ceeded in gaining permission to stretch a unit on the Harlem Renais-sance from three to nine days during the month of February; however, the school's standardized testing schedule required that Joann ultimately cut the unit to seven days. Factoring in the final essay assessment on the sev-enth day and an unexpected "day of silence" imposed by another teacher (more on this later), the time spent discussing the literature of the Harlem Renaissance took place over only five class sessions. As we began the unit I was a month into my fieldwork and had settled into my role of partici-pant observer, sometimes stationed at my computer, taking notes on class discussions, but often involving myself in small- and large-group conversa-tions. The students had also become used to my presence, and I was begin-ning to form bonds with some in this class; for example, when I was absent during the essay-writing assignment that took place on the final day of the Harlem Renaissance unit, Joann informed me that students had asked for me, and that Violet, especially, had "missed me." From that point on Violet was sure to scold me any time I was absent.[1]

During the first two days of the Harlem Renaissance unit, students listened to music and poetry recitations of the era, answering discussion questions and filling in worksheets. Although all of the artists under study were African American, the topic of racism was not specifically addressed until the third day, when Joann asked the class to discuss two poems by Langston Hughes: "I, Too," and "A Dream Deferred." Discussion surrounding the poems soon heated up as Joann tried to take students to a place where some did not want to go: acknowledging the focus of racism in the poetry of Hughes and the overall impact of racism on African Americans. Students resisted addressing these issues through two contextualized arguments that I will name "retrojection" and "this is all we ever talk about."

"I, Too"

Joann began class discussion on "I, Too" by pointing out Hughes's allusion to a Walt Whitman poem that the class had studied earlier in the school year, "I Hear America Singing." After asking the students to read "I, Too," Joann instructed the class to "discuss the issues of the poem, and tell why Hughes alludes to Whitman's work." Below are the two poems.

Henry Louis Gates Jr. (1988) explains the tradition of "signifying" in African American literature: "To name our tradition is to rename each of its antecedents, no matter how pale they might seem. To rename is to revise, and to revise is to Signify" (xxiii). Accordingly, in "I, Too," Hughes "signifies" Whitman, "challenging American rituals of incorporation and exclusion while more subtly playing off of Whitman's 'I Hear America Singing' with a dark minor chord" (Hutchinson 1992, 22). Therefore, Joann's instruction to compare the poems was in line with established scholarship.

Ron, a white student, spoke first, saying, "The two poems are different because Whitman's poem was talking about occupations, not races. Whitman very well may have been talking about African American or Puerto Rican construction workers." Anna (white) and Michelle (African American), sitting at Ron's table, agreed. Anna said of Hughes, "I think he agreed with Whitman. He used Whitman because he liked his work."

The students continued in this vein, agreeing that Whitman was part of the canon and Hughes would have known his poetry. Joann then steered the discussion toward the content of "I, Too," asking, "What is this poem about?"

I Hear America Singing

BY WALT WHITMAN

I hear America singing, the varied car-
    ols I hear,
Those of mechanics, each one sing-
    ing his as it should be blithe and
    strong,
The carpenter singing his as he mea-
    sures his plank or beam,
The mason singing his as he makes
    ready for work, or leaves off work,
The boatman singing what belongs to
    him in his boat, the deckhand sing-
    ing on the steamboat deck,
The shoemaker singing as he sits on
    his bench, the hatter singing as he
    stands,
The wood-cutter's song, the plough-
    boy's on his way in the morning,
    or at noon intermission or at
    sundown,
The delicious singing of the mother, or
    of the young wife at work, or of the
    girl sewing or washing,
Each singing what belongs to him or
    her and to none else,
The day what belongs to the day—at
    night the party of young fellows,
    robust, friendly,
Singing with open mouths their strong
    melodious songs.

I, Too

BY LANGSTON HUGHES

I, too, sing America.

I am the darker brother.
They send me to eat in the kitchen
When company comes,
But I laugh,
And eat well,
And grow strong.

Tomorrow,
I'll be at the table
When company comes.
Nobody'll dare
Say to me,
"Eat in the kitchen,"
Then.

Besides,
They'll see how beautiful I am
And be ashamed—

I, too, am America.

Students called out, "racism," "segregation," and "being sent out."

Violet, who was sitting with her friend Juliette (both African American), said seriously, "I don't hear America singing. I hear the white man singing."

Joann did not acknowledge Violet's comment, and students continued to discuss the connection between Whitman's and Hughes's work. I participated with students in the following discussion:

LAURA (white): He [Hughes] used Whitman's poem because people understand the allusion. They can connect to it.

MM: What about Ron's point that Whitman was talking about occupations, not races? Can we argue that he wasn't thinking about people of other races?

VIOLET (African American): It's inferred.

JULIETTE (African American): Because at that time African Americans weren't shoemakers or woodcutters. They were on plantations or in the fields.

MM: So sometimes what's left out of the text is as important as what's included in the text. Because of the time Whitman's poem was written, can we assume that he wasn't including African Americans?

LAURA: But I don't think Walt Whitman was racist. He helped black people. He fed them in his kitchen.

At the beginning of the class discussion of "I, Too," students recognized that through this poem Hughes was exploring the racism faced by African Americans of his day. However, Ron's initial comment ("Whitman's poem was talking about occupations, not races") showed his hesitancy to view the Whitman poem through the lens of critical race analysis, and set the stage for the conversation that followed. Perhaps because of Violet's implicit critique of Whitman's poem ("I don't hear America singing. I hear the white man singing"), which everyone heard but no one acknowledged, and my follow-up questions, students shifted the focus of their analysis away from the Hughes poem toward defending Whitman from perceived accusations of racism. When the class had studied Whitman's poetry earlier in the school year, Joann had introduced excerpts from "Song of Myself" as autobiographical. Laura's comment, "He helped black people. He fed them in his kitchen," referred to a portion of that poem that speaks of welcoming a runaway slave into the house through the kitchen and feeding him there. Ironically, in protecting Whitman's reputation, Laura nearly quoted a line from "I, Too," "Nobody'll dare / Say to me / 'Eat in the kitchen' / Then."

Unfortunately, neither Joann nor I noticed this at the time, and missed the opportunity to point out that relegation to the kitchen was exactly the expression of racism that Hughes's poem exposes. We did both state, however, that we were not implying that Whitman was outwardly racist, but we were questioning if, as a product of his time, Whitman's view of "America singing" included anyone other than whites. While Violet and Juliette nodded their approval, the rest of the class stared at us blankly. Our discussion of "I, Too" ended with some white students feeling defensive for the sake of a poet they had come to appreciate, Walt Whitman, and perhaps identifying with him as a white person accused of racism. We saw previously that many whites at EA, students and teachers alike, were anxious about perceived accusations of racism, and since Whitman was not there to defend himself, perhaps students felt they should defend him. While of course students are used to responding to questions about a text like the ones Joann and I presented in class that day, in retrospect I believe that the tenor of the discussion regarding Whitman's poem helped create the student responses that I explain below.

"A Dream Deferred"

The disagreement over Whitman's views on race that had caused some students to respond defensively seemed to carry over into discussion of the next Hughes poem, originally titled "Harlem," but referred to by Joann and the students as "A Dream Deferred." The students read the following poem from the handout that Joann had provided:

Harlem

BY LANGSTON HUGHES

What happens to a dream deferred?
Does it dry up
like a raisin in the sun?
Or fester like a sore—
And then run?
Does it stink like rotten meat?
Or crust and sugar over—
like a syrupy sweet?
Maybe it just sags
like a heavy load.
Or does it explode?[2]

Joann then asked the students to "discuss the poem" in small groups at their tables. She gave no other particular discussion guidelines or questions. The following is an excerpt of that discussion from my field notes:

I walk around, eventually settling at Violet's table. Violet is up, writing her group's ideas about the meaning of the poem on the board. I ask two white students, Emma and Edward, what they think the poem is about.

EMMA: It's about dreams and what happens when they're deferred. I don't think this has anything to do with being black.

Edward nods in agreement. I ask, "So you don't think Langston Hughes was writing about race?"

EMMA: No.

I can't think of any response, so I move on. At a table across the room two African American students, Juliette and Lyssa, say that the poem is about civil rights and social equality. Lyssa writes this on the board. However, a few minutes later during class discussion, Lyssa qualifies, "I don't think it [the poem] necessarily has to be about civil rights. I think he and lots of other African Americans had dreams about other things, and not just about civil rights."

JOANN: So, it's about a human experience, not just about civil rights?
LYSSA: Yeah.
JOANN: What if I tell you that the original title of the poem was, "Harlem, A Dream Deferred"? People have forgotten the original title. Does that change your reading of the poem?
MICHELLE (African American): He's not talking about equality. He's talking about talent.

I ask Michelle to explain further. She says, "He's telling people to pursue their talents, not to give up their dreams."

RON (white): Word.
MM (evenly): So in this poem Langston Hughes is talking to people who live in Harlem about their talents?

All nod in agreement.

ANTHONY (African American): He's talking about the place where he resides, like, the people there. He feels like they got shorthanded at times. He's asking the general public why this is.

EMMA (white): It's about what people are going through in that neighborhood.

VIOLET (African American): Just because it's by an African American author doesn't mean that they want civil rights.

LEAH (Chinese American): Changing the title doesn't change what we thought the poem was about, how everyone has different dreams . . . he was pondering what happens to dreams because he saw people having different reactions.

JOANN: I'm gonna play devil's advocate with this reading. Hughes is in Harlem. We know that the poem is about Harlem. He uses contrasting imagery like Billie Holiday does in "Strange Fruit." What does it mean that the last line of the poem is italicized? . . . One critic says it's a threat. Is it? Is it saying that if you ignore this, push away Harlem, segregate us, is this what's going to happen? Is it going to explode?

RON: You gonna shoot the place up?

JOANN: Maybe he didn't mean it literally? A critic can make the argument that it's a protest poem and he is threatening a society that is prejudiced . . . what do you think of that?

ANTHONY: I think it's fair. I mean it does make sense because he seems kind of bitter . . . he's using rotten meat and saying that it's shriveling up like a raisin . . . one day you're gonna get what's coming to you.

Joann asks the students to comment on why the last line of the poem is italicized.

RON: Maybe he just did it for a jolly.

MICHELLE: I italicize just for fun sometimes. I don't think it's a threat.

Perhaps because of feelings of defensiveness that had developed during the previous discussion, students were now closed to the idea of acknowledging the topic of race in "A Dream Deferred." White students, Emma, Edward, and Ron, had led the charge, but others, including African Americans, had followed along in arguing that Langston Hughes, an author who helped shape the civil rights movement, was not referring to racism in one of his most widely known and vividly worded poems.

While Emma and Edward were adamant in this belief from the start, African American students showed a gradual adoption of their white classmates' opinions as the class period progressed. For example, at the beginning of the lesson Lyssa agreed with Juliette (both African American) that "A Dream Deferred" was a poem about "civil rights and social equality," and wrote this on the board. However, during the large-group discussion that followed shortly after, Lyssa qualified this statement with the words, "I don't think it necessarily *has* to be about civil rights. I think he and lots of other African Americans had dreams about other things, and not just about civil rights." Anthony's reflection that the poem was about how people in Harlem had been "shorthanded" (I believe he meant to say, "shortchanged") implied that racism was involved, but Emma mitigated Anthony's implication when she said, "It's about what people are going through in that neighborhood," and Anthony did not disagree. Emma localized Hughes's intended audience to one neighborhood to imply that it was not meant as a more general critique of racism. Even Violet, who had earlier commented, "I don't hear America singing. I hear the white man singing," eventually agreed that "Just because it's by an African American author doesn't mean that they want civil rights." Michelle aligned herself with Ron in trivializing Hughes's choice to italicize the last line of the poem, "*Or does it explode.*" Juliette, who just two days previously had announced, snapping her fingers, "I'd change Black History Month—I'd make it two months! So there!" and who had been quite vocal at the beginning of this class period, had lapsed into silence by its end. Only Anthony was willing to admit that a protest reading of the poem was "fair." Thus, African American students like Violet and Juliette, who had at first seemed eager to explore the themes of racism in the Hughes's poems, found themselves "disabled from influencing others" (Lueck and Steffen 2011, 49) and simply gave up.

That day at lunch I shared with Joann my surprise at the students' responses to Hughes's poetry. Of course, teachers encourage students to make their own meanings from the literature they read, and I am not suggesting that the Hughes poems we studied that day were only about race or that broader interpretations of these works are not valid. Literary critics have argued the relative significance of authorial intent for decades, and it is not within the scope of this study to explore that issue. Since Joann's unit was tied to the historicity of racism, students' understanding of Hughes's intent in writing these two poems was an important element of her lesson. However, it was not students' belief that "A Dream Deferred" may be applied broadly to the human experience of disappointment in unfulfilled dreams that surprised me. Rather, what surprised me was students' insistence that Hughes was not writing about the effects of racism on African Americans during the time period in which the poem was written, illustrated by Emma's statement, "I don't think this has anything to do with being black."

During our lunchtime conversation, Joann suggested the term "retrojection" to describe the discourse that students had engaged in that morning. Retrojection is the practice of interpreting past events through the lens of present sensibilities.[3] Joann remembered the term from a college literature course she had taken, and I thought it an accurate description of what we had heard from students that day. Students had analyzed a Langston Hughes poem written during the civil rights movement through the lens of their beliefs about present-day racism.

A few weeks later I had the chance to talk further with Anthony about the class discussion of the Hughes poem. He had plopped himself down in the cushy green armchair next to my little desk in the corner of the room, and we chatted for a few minutes between activities.

MM: Remember when people thought that Langston Hughes wasn't writing about race?

ANTHONY: Yeah, I was one of them.

M: So you think, with the way things were back then, that he wasn't writing about race?

A: [nods] I think he was writing for his hometown, for the people who lived there.

M: He didn't have a broader audience in mind?

A: [shakes head] Nope. He was just writing for the people around him.

M: So do you think things were the same then as they are now?

A: [nods] Basically, just like people today, he wanted to be liked by the people around him, in his hometown.

M: By hometown do you mean Harlem?

A: [nods] Just like today, he knew the people around him, and that's who he was writing for.

M: You don't think he was writing about race?

A: Nope. He was just writing for his hometown.

Again, I was surprised by Anthony's responses. Although he had been the only student to agree that a protest reading of "A Dream Deferred" was "fair," during our private conversation he pulled back from this position and adopted more fully the interpretations of his friends.

Puzzled and wanting to hear from more students about this, several weeks later during my interview with Anna, a white student, I asked if she thought Hughes had been writing about race in "A Dream Deferred."

> ANNA: Yeah, but I think that my class doesn't see it as that because of how things are now, and they don't compare it to then and now.
>
> MM: So why do you think that is?
>
> ANNA: 'Cause they're used to [laughs], they're used to just being, like, open, and, especially at this school, because everyone is, like, really ethnically mixed.... Where at, like, a normal public school it's not, so maybe you would think about it more as a race thing. Rather than here, it's not.

Anna, who had disagreed with other students but had remained silent that day in class, believed that her classmates' understanding of present race relations hinders them from acknowledging racism in the past ("my class doesn't see it as that because of how things are now"). Further, Anna described the atmosphere at EA as "open," and I believe her use of the term, "ethnically mixed" refers not to individual student's mixed racial/ethnic backgrounds but to the prevalence of cross-racial friendships at the school. Anna believed that students' cross-racial friendships stopped them from needing to think about race, as if these friendships are proof that racism does not exist at the school. At a "normal public school" where, presumably, students are not so friendly toward one another, students might be more likely to explore the theme of racism in the Hughes poetry, but at EA students' close cross-racial friendships make this unnecessary.

During our interview, which took place more than three months after we had discussed "A Dream Deferred" in class, Anthony told me that, after thinking more about it, he had changed his opinion about the poem. He admitted, "I guess it could make sense that he [Hughes] was, maybe, talking about race." When I asked him why he thought his classmates had been so adamantly opposed to the idea, he offered, "I guess because we weren't living in that time, so we really don't have a good understanding, that we just believe, ok, he's just talking about everybody, because we see everybody as the same." Anthony speaks of himself and his classmates as a cohesive group that is nonracist and colorblind ("we see everybody as the same") and that is too far removed from past racism to understand it ("I guess because we weren't living in that time"). Like Anna, he believes that students' nonracist positioning in the present makes them less inclined to discuss racism in the past. While students remained firm in their use of retrojection that day, when challenged through the next day's class discussion, they shifted to the use of a new argument.

"This Is All We Ever Talk About"

The day after our analysis of the Hughes's poems, Joann decided to debrief with the students about the previous class. During that class discussion, white students shifted their argument from retrojection to complaints of how frequently the class talked about racism.

> JOANN: This is something I want to open up to your class specifically. There's this interesting hesitation, almost resistance to talking about certain issues in here, almost as if, if we don't talk about them they won't exist.... We're talking about Harlem, race riots, people who are impacted by race every day. This class doesn't seem to want to look at it from that lens. It's almost like because today it's not an issue, we look back and say that it wasn't an issue then.
>
> EMMA: I feel like I don't have the historical context, so I can't really talk about it. Also, I want to look at poetry from the point of the issues of the author as a human being and not just a black person.
>
> EDWARD: [sitting across from Emma] We already know the issues, we just keep talking about what we already know over and over.... We already know that Harlem had racism problems.... We already talk about it so much that there's nothing else to say.
>
> JOANN: Is that how everyone feels? I really am interested. I really want to hear your voices.

Lots of nodding and murmuring in agreement. Juliette and Anthony are silent and Violet is absent.

> CATHY: I've gone over and over this again and again. We understand that there was racism. We're just tired of talking about it over and over again.
>
> JOANN: So you've talked about it so much that it's lost its value?

Again students nod in agreement, murmuring, "Yes."

Thus, Joann introduced this discussion by reinforcing the idea that racism no longer exists, an idea that, through my many conversations with her, I know she did not believe. Yet, perhaps because of her own discomfort with the topic, in this instance she adopted this softer approach.

Emma and Edward (who were sitting together) objected to discussions of racism through contradicting arguments. Although Joann confirmed to me that Emma and Edward had been in the same honors history classes throughout high school and had studied the same historical facts regarding the history of race in the United States, Emma stated that she doesn't know enough about the historical context of the poems to explore themes of racism within them, while Edward implied that he knows about the issue of racism so thoroughly that there is nothing left to talk about. Emma employed colorblind ideology in her argument as well; she wanted to look at Hughes as a human being, she said, and not just as a black man. In separating Hughes from his blackness, Emma normalizes whiteness, wanting to ascribe Hughes the same raceless status that whites often ascribe themselves (Marx 2006; McIntyre 1997). Ignoring Hughes's racial background as she analyzes his poetry would allow Emma to avoid discussing the racism that was so prevalent during the time that the poet wrote. Therefore, Emma's attempt to remake Hughes in her own likeness (as raceless) enables her to avoid thinking about racism. While listening to Emma I could not help but wonder if she would have thought of saying of Walt Whitman, "I want to look at poetry from the point of the issues of the author as a human being and not just a white person."

Although the previous day was the first time they had discussed racism during this unit and only the second time in the month that I had been at the school, other students aligned themselves with Edward's complaint and maintained that the class had spent too much time on the topic. The students' shift in discourse from retrojection to a new argument ("this is all we ever talk about") is significant because it makes clear that students actually did know that racism existed during the time that Hughes was writing. Students' use of retrojection was not born of a lack of factual information. When Joann challenged this discourse ("It's almost like because today it's not an issue, we look back and say that it wasn't an issue then"), students took up a new argument to bolster their resistance, complaining they had been overexposed to the topic of racism. However, I was to discover that students' complaints of overexposure did not apply to another subject within the school's curriculum: the Holocaust.

Privileging of the Holocaust

The next day, a Friday, the eleventh grade students were buzzing about the "day of silence" activity scheduled by Mr. Jay, their history teacher, for the coming Monday. Mr. Jay had explained that, because of students' strong interest in studying the Holocaust, his eleventh grade class would remain silent for the entire school day. This, he hoped, would help students to imagine the experience of Anne Frank and others who hid to escape the Nazis.

Joann was surprised by the "day of silence" activity since the eleventh grade students had studied the Holocaust the year before and were supposed to be studying American history this year. In light of students' complaints that they were sick of discussing the same issues over and over again, I wondered how they would react to repeating their study of the Holocaust for the second year in a row. I floated from table to table that morning, asking students how they felt about the day of silence activity. Surprisingly, most students felt positively about the assignment.

I asked, "So you've studied all this before, right? You don't mind doing it again?"

Edward acknowledged that they had learned about the Holocaust the previous year, but he was willing to participate in Mr. Jay's activity because "it's the respectable thing to do."

Ruthie (a white student and a close friend of Edward) explained, "Every time you do it you see it from a different angle. You go into it deeper."

Emma and the other white students at her table were also very positive about observing the day of silence. They, too, admitted that they had studied the Holocaust before but said, "It's fine because this will be a deeper experience." The very same students who had complained that they were tired of talking about racism toward African Americans were not at all tired of discussing the Holocaust and were even willing to forgo communicating with their friends for an entire school day in order to "go deeper" into the topic. Apparently these students did not feel that revisiting the subject of racism experienced by African Americans had the same benefit.

Preliminary Thoughts

As I tried to make sense of students' responses, it seemed unlikely that eleventh grade honors students' resistance to discussing racism was due to boredom or lack of historical context. Rather, their responses to the Hughes poems indicated the workings of simultaneous processes in students' thinking. It seems likely that some students were annoyed at Joann and me because they perceived our comments about Walt Whitman during our comparison of "I, Too" with "I Hear America Singing" as accusations of racism. Students may have felt the need to speak for Whitman, who can no longer speak for himself. It is also possible that Joann's assurance "I really am interested. I really want to hear your voices" had given students the false impression that their opinions would be respected and the class would not discuss racism again. If so, students' frustration at being ignored is understandable. However, inseparable from their irritation with us (and perhaps partly the reason for that irritation) was a racial identity that was uncomfortable acknowledging past and present racism. It is impossible to tease out how much of students' denial of the racism theme in Hughes's work was about resisting the voices of the two adults in the room and how much was an effort to avoid grappling with the challenging subject of racism. In any case, by the end of the Harlem Renaissance unit, students were actively developing unique, contextualized discourses to help them avoid talking about racism.

Ironically, for some students the seeds of frustration and resentment were sown through discussion of texts that were meant to broaden students' understandings of the devastating effects of racism. These students would grow more vocal in their objections in the coming days. At the same time, some African American students began to develop the habit of silence in the face of their friends' resentment. The next chapter explores more fully the mixture of anger and silence that came to characterize the responses of this "friendly" eleventh grade group.

4

Resistance among Friends

■ ■ ■ ■ ■ ■ ■ ■ ■ ■ ■ ■ ■ ■ ■ ■ ■

The Bluest Eye

The eleventh grade honors class began studying Toni Morrison's (1970) novel *The Bluest Eye* at the end of April, approximately ten weeks after we had finished the Harlem Renaissance unit. By that time I was nearing the end of my fieldwork and had become somewhat of a semipermanent fixture in Joann's classes. While most students felt comfortable enough to include me in their jokes when they were in the mood and ignore me when they weren't, an interesting dynamic had developed in my student relationships. Some of the white students who had worked to avoid discussing race in our analysis of the Hughes poems now seemed to steer clear of me as much as possible, interacting with a cool but polite detachment when I joined their small group discussions. Ron and James, for example, no longer bantered with me about being Italian American and now and then exchanged glances when I commented during class discussions. At the same time, I had established a warm friendliness with Violet, Juliette, and Anthony. Violet and Anthony, in particular, often sat near me or motioned for me to join their group, and one day I returned from the ladies' room to find the two of them hovering near my desk, looking around with confused expressions. They seemed relieved when they saw me, and explained their confusion: they knew I was present because they saw my belongings, but they didn't know where I had gone. We laughed and I told them that next time I would ask them to sign my agenda book before leaving the room (as students were required to do).

Although the class had not discussed racism at all since the final day of the Harlem Renaissance unit, many of the same contextualized arguments that students developed during that unit resurfaced with greater potency in our discussions of *The Bluest Eye*. Set during the Great Depression, the novel tells several interconnecting stories of African American characters through the eyes of the child protagonist, Claudia. Claudia and her older sister, Frieda, watch helplessly as their good friend, Pecola, victimized by a racist society and abused by her father, eventually descends into madness. We studied *The Bluest Eye* for one month, missing some days for standardized testing and a field trip. The bulk of the unit focused on the damaging effects of "white beauty standards" on the characters; this was the topic of both a final collage and an essay assignment. During the last few class sessions of the unit, Joann, borrowing course materials that I had used over the years with college students, showed the students episode three of the California Newsreel video *Race: The Power of an Illusion* (2003), which details housing discrimination after World War II. On the final day of the unit students discussed the widely used Peggy McIntosh (2005) essay "White Privilege: Unpacking the Invisible Knapsack."

Reemergence of Discourses

From the outset, students' responses to *The Bluest Eye* were divided along the lines of race. The same white students who were vocal in their displeasure of discussing racism in the poems of Langston Hughes were equally vocal in their dislike of Morrison's text. In fact, dissention over the novel started even before we began the unit, perhaps because students who had clearly stated they were tired of talking about race during the Harlem Renaissance unit felt the added frustration of having their opinions ignored. While Violet and Juliette told me that they were excited about reading *The Bluest Eye*, some white students were annoyed from the outset that the Morrison novel would replace *The Catcher in the Rye* for their class.

"Why can't we read a book that everyone has heard of?" Cathy complained.

"People have heard of *The Bluest Eye*!" Juliette responded indignantly. Thus, the stage was set, and this initial resentment grew in many students as we progressed through the reading of the novel.

The Return of "This Is All We Ever Talk About"

A few days into *The Bluest Eye* unit, I settled at a discussion group where white students Ron, James, Emma, and Edward sat at one end of the table and African American students Lyssa, Violet, and Lucky, who remained silent for almost the whole discussion, sat at the other. A conversation ensued about how much students disliked the novel.

> RON: This is my least favorite book ever. I'd like to deconstruct the text [makes motion like he is ripping a book in half and throwing it away].

Ron's comment referred to a lesson on literary deconstruction that Joann had presented a few days previously. The discussion continued:

> RON: All of this happened long before we were born. We can't relate to it. How are we supposed to get past racism if we keep talking about it?
> VIOLET: [quietly] Calm down, best friend.

Violet and Ron often greeted each other with a warm, "Hello, best friend," sometimes followed by a hug. Yet, throughout the unit Ron seemed completely unaware of how his words might impact his African American "best friend." I decided to join in.

> MM: So you don't like this book?
> JAMES: [motioning at Ron] He doesn't like books that deal with these kinds of issues.
> RON: Why don't we talk about more modern issues of oppression?
> MM: Like what?
> RON: Well, like gay rights. That's more relevant in today's world.
> EDWARD: I don't understand why we have to keep talking about this over and over again. I'm tired of talking about things that happened in the past that don't affect us. It's not preparing us.

MM: Preparing you for what? For college? For life?

EDWARD: For college or for life.

MM: If you had your choice, what kinds of things would you read in school?

EDWARD: Stephen King.

EMMA: This is all we ever talk about in lit class. Talking about it just makes it worse. Why can't we ever just read a book for the story? Why do we always have to talk about these issues? Why can't we just talk about what the book is actually about?

VIOLET: But racism *is* what this book is about.

Students ignore Violet's comment. They continue to complain about the text.

EMMA: Talking about racism and sexism makes it worse. We can't get past it if we keep talking about it. Why do we have to talk about sexism if it doesn't exist any more?

EDWARD: It's ironic. They want us to stop being racist but they keep talking about it. The way to stop something is to stop giving it attention.

EMMA: I, personally, have never experienced sexism. I have never been kept from doing something because I'm a girl.

Emma's comment might reflect the impatience she and other students had shown toward Joann's feminist reading of *The Scarlet Letter* earlier in the school year. She and others had claimed that there was no longer any need to talk about the oppression of women in the past because women had fully achieved equal rights in the present. Thus, these students conflated sexism and racism as issues that no longer affect them.

James affirmed Emma's comment by saying, "Yeah, women make a little less money than men, but other than that, sexism doesn't exist, unless I'm misinformed. And Ron, Edward, and I are white males. We've never experienced anything like this, so we can't relate to it at all."

Once again, the idea that racism no longer exists (an idea that Joann had inadvertently reinforced during the Harlem Renaissance unit) acted as a springboard for students' complaints. Infused in students' arguments were two essential features of whiteness discourse that continued throughout the remainder of the unit:[1] the refusal to recognize the broad scope of present racism and the downplaying of the lasting effects of racism in the past (Leonardo 2002).

During this conversation, students expanded their "this is all we ever talk about" argument in several ways. Ron noted that the topic of racism is not relevant the way a more up-to-date topic, such as gay rights, might be. His desire to discuss "more modern issues of oppression" illustrates his construction of racism as an issue of the past. Edward agreed with and elaborated on Ron's view by adding that the issue doesn't affect them; his view of racism as individual acts of discrimination allows him to avoid thinking about himself or his white friends as the beneficiaries of a racist system (Flynn 2012). Although they had studied slavery and the civil rights movement in previous years, Edward and the other white students in this class had never been asked to consider their privileged position as whites and were therefore able to think of themselves as unaffected by the issue of racism. Heather Lewis-Charp (2003) studied white students at six multiracial high schools and found that, since school curriculum centered on slavery, the civil rights movement, the treatment of Native Americans, and the Holocaust, students were "not exposed to a complex examination of movements for social change" (283) and, like white students at EA, developed the neoliberal view that racism is no longer an issue. Not surprisingly, white students who had not considered their own position of racial dominance were unable to examine racism in all its forms through a critical lens (McIntyre 1997).

While Edward's desire to read Stephen King novels in school may also reflect a wish for less challenging, more entertaining curriculum that may be common among students, he also argues that a text about racism is irrelevant and does not help to prepare students for the future. James extends Edward's argument with his comment that white males cannot be expected to relate to a book that does not explore the experience of white males (Beach, Thein, and Parks 2008). In a variation of the color-blind argument known as "racial evasion" (Bucholtz 2011, 169), Edward and Emma agree that talking about racism makes it worse, and that the way to end racism is to ignore it. All of these arguments were made quite loudly while the African American students at the other end of the table remained silent, with the exception of Violet's quiet defense, "But racism *is* what this book is about." This pattern of silence from African American students was to grow stronger as discussion of racism continued.

Making a *Night* of It

A few minutes later, James reminisced about a book they had read the year before that he had really appreciated, the 1958 Elie Wiesel memoir, *Night*. He had enjoyed that one, he said, and didn't mind talking about race in that book because *Night* was a book he could relate to. Ron agreed, stating, "Yeah, if I'd realized earlier that it was an actual experience, I could have related to it even more. By the time I realized it we were almost finished with the book. We need to read more books about real experiences."[2]

Of this very vocal group of white students, only James agreed to be interviewed by me. Our interview took place a few days later, and I asked James about his feeling that as a white male he couldn't relate to the Morrison text. I suggested that perhaps literature is important because through it we can experience situations that we will never experience in real life. James (diplomatic as always) replied that, although I'd made a good point,

> . . . the huge difference in life between me and the main character, from what I'm seeing in the first couple of chapters, is substantial to the point where I'm having a hard time, you know, not even relating to it, just, you know, believing it. Because, you know, the way that she's treated by these people is something that, you know, I, I didn't know people could be treated that badly. So, I guess one of the big reasons why I can't relate to it as well is because, you know, I'm not seeing the reality in it.

Here, James expands his argument: the problem is not just that he, as a white male, cannot relate to the racism faced by the characters in the novel, the problem is that he doesn't actually believe that the story could have happened to anyone. In another moment of retrojection, James sends his belief that racism is over back through time, stating that he is "not seeing the reality" of the text: that is, the depictions of racism in the text cannot possibly be thought of as real. James then clarifies his point by mentioning *Night* again, explaining why he enjoyed it so much more than *The Bluest Eye*: "It's a firsthand account, written by a Holocaust survivor of, you know, the concentration camps, uh, used by the Nazis. It was kind of hard to, you know, not believe in that, because the guy lived it, you know. Which is why it's easier to believe in the truth than it is to believe in realistic fiction."

I came away from my interview with James perplexed. Why did he have so much trouble believing a story that depicted white racism toward African Americans, yet value so deeply accounts of European anti-Semitism? Was his fiction/nonfiction dichotomy solely responsible? James's disbelief that events of *The Bluest Eye* were possible may indicate that reading the text placed him in an uncomfortable position of conflict. Helms (1990) posits that when whites' beliefs of racial equity are first challenged, they become aware of the moral dilemmas associated with being white and may experience guilt and anxiety. Not wanting to believe in whites' societal advantage, they experience cognitive dissonance, an uncomfortable state that they will attempt to reduce. One method of reducing dissonance, according to Helms, is to seek confirmations that "either racism is not the White person's fault or does not really exist" (59). James's admission, "I didn't know people could be treated that badly," shows the dissonance the events of the story caused him; his response, "I'm not seeing the reality in it," shows his attempt to reduce that dissonance by invalidating the text.

"I'm Not German"

During my interview with Anthony I asked him why he thought his white classmates complained that they had talked about racism toward blacks too much but never seemed to tire of talking about the Holocaust. Anthony replied, "Maybe it's because they weren't directly responsible." When I asked him to clarify, he role-played the position his white friends might take: "'I'm not German. It's not my fault.' . . . I can look at it objectively and analyze exactly what's going on here. But, I mean, if we're talking about slavery . . . I wouldn't want to talk about slavery all the time if I was white, because I would feel, well, like, these are my ancestors that did this, and I feel kind of bad about this." Anthony believed that his white friends were defensive about the topic of American slavery because they felt guilty (Helms 1990) knowing that their ancestors were responsible for the atrocities committed against African Americans. No such guilt existed regarding the Holocaust, which freed white students to fully explore the topic objectively. Again putting himself in the place of his white classmates, Anthony explained, "I'm not German, and this [the Holocaust] is actually interesting, what happened. Like, the thing is interesting." Therefore, James's choice to distrust the story of *The Bluest Eye*, brushing it off as merely fiction, absolves him of the guilt he and other whites may experience as they grapple with the stark reality of racism in their own country, while his affinity for the victims of the Holocaust allows him to adopt the position of a caring, empathetic, and nonracist person. In choosing to favor study of the Holocaust over that of American racism, James protects both his image and his emotional interests as a white person.

White Beauty Standards: Patterns of Interaction

Much of the class discussion that took place over the next few weeks focused on the damaging effects of white standards of beauty experienced by the characters in *The Bluest Eye*. A pattern of student interaction emerged as students engaged in curricular activities: many of the white students continued to resist acknowledging racism while African American students either agreed with them or, for the majority of the unit, were silent. Leah, a Chinese American student, sat with white students and rarely spoke in a large-group setting on any topic; therefore, it is difficult to know if her silence regarding racism was indicative of her racial identity or a product of a quiet personality. Students began to self-segregate more as discussions about race grew intense, and Lyssa and Michelle, the two light-skinned African American females in the class, almost always aligned themselves with the vocal white students both physically (in terms of seating) and attitudinally (in denying the existence of racism and white privilege). Until the last day or two of the unit, Anthony, Violet, Juliette, Lucky, and Karla, the darker-skinned African Americans, were either silent or incredibly diplomatic in their comments. Other white students also chose to remain silent.

The tendency for light-skinned African Americans to side with whites might be seen as a form of colorism, discrimination based on skin color among members of the same racial group (Perry 2011; Winkler 2012). Ironically, this tendency became most evident during the unit on *The Bluest Eye* when students viewed *A Girl Like Me*, a documentary by teen filmmaker Kiri Davis (2007) that explores the harmful emotional effects of white beauty standards on darker-skinned black girls. Some students responded to the documentary by reinforcing rather than problematizing (as the film meant to do) the message that when it comes to hair and skin color, the closer the approximation of whiteness, the better. For example, Lyssa commented that the film was "true," but rather than explore the film's theme of discrimination, she simply stated, "That's why I relax my hair." About her skin color she said, "I'm light-skinned, so that's not an issue." Neither Joann, nor I, nor any of the other students challenged Lyssa's normalization of the emotionally damaging situation that Davis portrayed in the film.

As the class then discussed the absence of dark-skinned African American models in beauty advertisements, Michelle commented, "It depends on the person—how much the person wants to work toward that. It's not a gender or race thing." Relying on development models of black racial identity, Helms (1990) explains that due to "advantaged status in their own racial group" (23) some African Americans may, without fully realizing it, ally themselves with whites in minimizing the impact of racism in order to maintain their higher status within their own group. For some, this status may come through lighter skin or straighter hair. The within-group bias of colorism can have serious emotional and economic effects and impacts socialization processes within families as much as traits like birth order or gender (Burton et al. 2010). Because of attitudes of colorism that have existed in the United States and around the world for centuries, Lyssa and Michelle's light skin grants them advantage that they are likely not aware of and makes their alignment with the white students in the class understandable. Perhaps this, in part, explains why Michelle did not state her belief that "racism will always exist because it's such a huge part of society" until the final day of *The Bluest Eye* unit. The darker-skinned African American females in the class agreed with the perspective of the filmmaker but did not elaborate on their feelings about the topic. Karla, for example, said of the Davis video, "It's true," but did not further express her opinion.

Some of the white students, however, had more to say. Edward complained about having "Jewish features" and "the Jew curl," stating that he "wasn't crazy about" this look. Edward's point was that white people, too, might be dissatisfied with their "ethnic" appearance; through his comments he identified himself as a victim of white beauty standards and minimized the effect that these standards have on people of color. From there students discussed what it meant to "look Italian" and the irony that whites tan to make their skin look darker. When Edward and the white students at his table turned the attention on themselves, they appropriated the struggle the girls in the film had expressed. Violet sat with them and listened quietly as the focus of the group discussion shifted away from her experience. As reported in similar settings (Beach, Thein, and Parks 2008; Naidoo 1992), in 11 Honors, members of the dominant culture often controlled discussions of race, effectively sidelining and silencing members of less powerful groups.

On another day, Joann asked the class to discuss *The Bluest Eye*'s main character, Claudia's, violent response to a Shirley Temple doll. Rather than treasuring the doll as other girls in the novel do, Claudia destroys it. The class discussed Morrison's association of physical beauty with whiteness, a main theme of the novel. Ron had this to say on the topic: "There was nothing intentional. I doubt that Shirley Temple was being raised as a child star just to spite the minorities. It seems like they're mentally putting that upon themselves. They just can't get over it." To Ron, the characters in the novel who "just can't get over it" are at fault, not the system of oppression under which they suffered. When Joann answered that the damage of white-dominated beauty standards may not have been intentional but nevertheless did happen, Ron continued sarcastically: "Well, pardon me for not being from that time period, and not being a little African American girl. Where's their pride? Can't they just look in a mirror or something and say, 'I'm beautiful'?" Here, Ron revisits the idea that as a white male he cannot be expected to relate to the experience of "a little African American girl" from a past time period. However, at the core of his comment is an impatience and intolerance toward the novel's African American characters. Naidoo (1992) noted white students' lack of sympathy for African American characters during a unit on *Roll of Thunder, Hear My Cry*, and Lewis-Charp (2003) found that white students' inclinations to view racism as a past problem "were often accompanied by a tendency to dismiss the experiences of other groups and, in some cases, blame people of color for their own social position" (283). These white students believed that people of color want to be seen as victims. Their narrow, ahistorical view of racism resulted in a lack of empathy very much like that expressed by Ron, who showed no awareness of the impact his harsh words might have on the students of color in his class—among them, his friend Violet.

After exchanging looks with Juliette, Violet, who was sitting at Ron's table, responded to Ron's questions, "Where's their pride? Can't they just look in a mirror or something and say, 'I'm beautiful'?" with the quiet but serious statement, "I'm black and I'm proud." She did not directly address Ron's attack of the black character in the novel, nor did she acknowledge his impatience and insensitivity. Although, by her statement, Violet expressed pride in her heritage, she avoided challenging Ron's insensitive rant by not defending Morrison's text directly. Further, she separated herself from the characters, implying, *yes, those characters should be black and proud like I am.* From her comment one might infer that Violet is not one of those blacks who, in Ron's view, "just can't get over it." By her words Violet positioned herself as an African American who would be a safe friend for a white person like Ron, who prefers to deny the existence of racism. Reciprocally, Ron's construction of how African Americans should respond to racism is informed by Violet's positioning. If Violet, black and proud, is able to "get over" the racism inherent in beauty standards that elevate whiteness, why can't other blacks do the same?

Of all the African American students in 11 Honors, Lucky, who did not boast close friendships with others in the class, was the most outspoken on the topic of racism in general and of white beauty standards in particu-lar. But even he mitigated the effects of present-day racism in discussing the child character Claudia's rage toward the Shirley Temple doll. Lucky explained, "She grew up witnessing the effect of white beauty standards on the two older girls, and that's what makes her angry. It's not like for us . . . we haven't experienced racism."

As I have mentioned previously, during our interview a few weeks later, Lucky again claimed he had never experienced racism but then changed his mind after he had thought about it more deeply. At that point he named specific examples of how he, his family members, and other African Ameri-can students at the school felt they had been discriminated against. Dur-ing class discussions, Lucky's stance on the issue was often conflicted. He did speak up at times, including a few days later, when he disagreed with Edward's statement that "If you're a minority among a group of others who are the majority, discrimination is just natural. All people have experienced discrimination in some form." Lucky replied, "White people aren't going to be followed around in Abercrombie." However, at other times Lucky either claimed he'd never experienced racism or took a low profile during class discussions.

Perhaps because of his close friendships with many white students in this class, Anthony's comments during class discussion were usually mea-sured and diplomatic, and he seemed to take pains to appear fair in his responses. For example, instead of objecting to Edward's claim that all peo-ple (including whites) experience racism, as Lucky did, Anthony agreed with Edward, saying, "Some people may think they're the only cool ones, and that if you're not like them, you're not cool." Anthony did not men-tion race in this response, but it was clear that he, like white tenth grader Tom, viewed exclusion from "coolness" status to be a form of discrimina-tion toward whites.

Similarly, it was during class discussion of white beauty standards that—in response to James's statement, "Some people are too sensitive"—Anthony tried to explain why black students might be "sensitive" about race through the "yellow posters" analogy described in chapter 2. By talking about posters instead of people, Anthony avoided mentioning the specific racial backgrounds of the people in the room, and his use of humor broke the tension that was building during class discussion. Through this and other interactions, Anthony made it a point to show sensitivity toward his white friends while still working to help them to see racism from his and other African American students' perspectives. While most of the class showed appreciation for Anthony's humor with laughter and smiles, based on their angry responses over the remaining classes in *The Bluest Eye* unit, it did not seem that they incorporated his perspective into their understanding of race relations. During the discussion that continued after Anthony's example of the "yellow posters," Joann told me that she had been standing near Ron and decided to count how many times he murmured "Oh, God" with his head down in his arms. She said she stopped counting at number eleven.

The same patterns of student interaction persisted on the day that students viewed each other's culminating "Beauty Standards Project," collages they had made of Internet and magazine ads that showed the representation of beauty in advertisements. Almost all students had included images of African Americans in their collages, but not one of them was dark-skinned, and all had straight or loosely curled hair. Joann asked the students if, based on their projects, they felt we have now overcome the racialization that the characters in the novel faced because of the internalization of white standards of beauty. Students responded:

EMMA (white): Yes. Look at Beyoncé. No one would ever say she's not beautiful.

EDWARD (white): I think there's an equal representation. In magazines, on billboards, there's not only white people. It's not necessarily equal representation, but it's not totally unequal.

LYSSA (light-skinned African American): It's just that there are more white people that are models.

MM: Why do you think that is?

LYSSA: If more African Americans wanted to be models, then they would be. It's their choice.

EMMA: There's plenty of representation.

DANA (white): If you look at the global world, there's equal representation.

While none of the students recognized the absence of dark-skinned African Americans in their collages, I found most significant the responses of Lyssa, a light-skinned African American, and Dana, a close friend of Juliette and Violet who, according to Joann, by her own admission, "only dated black guys." In the case of these two females, neither insider status nor close friendship ties with African Americans allowed them to consider that racism might be responsible for the absence of dark-skinned models in media. At the heart of their statements lie the essential discourses of whiteness: reluctance to acknowledge the continuing existence of racism and a tendency to underestimate the lasting effects of racism that occurred in the past (Frankenberg 1993; Gillborn 2009; Leonardo 2002; Roediger 1992).

And so it went. Day after day the same white students dominated class discussions, becoming more and more angry and resistant to the notion of present-day racism. The vocal white students employed similar tactics as those described by Alice McIntyre (1997), using variations of "white talk" (45) to resist conversations of race. They dominated the discourse with their complaints, dismissed the experiences of African American students and the arguments Joann and I offered, and showed disinterest by whispering and laughing during class discussion. Other white students remained silent, and the African American students, with a few exceptions, either agreed with the vocal white students or also remained silent. Ron took to carrying a metal kitchen teaspoon with him, waving it around during class discussions and motioning as if he were feeding himself. He exclaimed often and loudly, "I have a spoon. I'm ready to be fed my daily dose of liberal nonsense." Even when Joann shared income, housing, or incarceration statistics that evidenced institutional racism, students remained silent or stubbornly opposed.

Joann and I hoped that two vehicles that had prompted productive discussion over many years with my college students, episode three of the California Newsreel video *Race: The Power of an Illusion* (2003), titled "The House We Live In," and the McIntosh (2005) white privilege essay, might help to broaden students' perspectives about the history of discrimination and white privilege in the United States. These were the topics of the final two days spent on *The Bluest Eye* unit.

Anger in the "House"

"The House We Live In" (2003) describes the complicity of the U.S. government and the mortgage industry in creating discriminatory housing policy after World War II and the devastating effect this policy has had on African Americans. Critical race theorists argue that attaining rights for African Americans has been an uphill battle because, from its inception, the United States has based individual rights on property ownership and not on human rights. They explain that since the signing of the Constitution, social benefits have always been given to property owners (Bell 1987; Harris 1993; Ladson-Billings and Tate 1995; Perry 2011). "The House We Live In" details how, more recently, whites were encouraged to purchase property and granted low-interest mortgages while African Americans were kept out of suburbia and relegated to public housing in urban centers. When blacks did purchase suburban homes, whites swiftly fled, creating lower property values and a lower tax base in African American neighborhoods, and, since public schools are largely funded through real estate taxes, a lower quality education for African American children. Ironically, EA owes its existence partly to these past policies since many of its students travel over an hour each way by bus to avoid attending Carltonville High, where the school's standardized test scores in all curriculum areas as well as the school's graduation rates are below state averages.

As the video played, some of the white students who had been the most resistant to conversations about racism showed their disinterest by whispering and laughing. When the video ended, Joann asked the students to share their gut reactions. Violet spoke first, saying that she was not surprised because her grandparents had experienced housing discrimination and had talked to her about it. After a long silence, Emma, Cathy, and Edward said that they, too, were not surprised by the facts of the video because they had "learned about it" in history class. More silence followed. Ron motioned as if being fed with his spoon (which he had drilled a hole in and now wore around his neck every day).

Then Joann asked a question: "Do you feel that the purpose of the video is to blame you?"

Many of the white students in the class exclaimed a resounding "Yes!" They continued, speaking over each other in rapid fire:

I feel like we're being blamed!

It's saying that we're all racist!

So this is all our fault!

Ron said, "Am I supposed to take the blame for my ancestors being allowed to buy a house?" I pointed out that one of the speakers in the video, Beverly Daniel Tatum, stated that none of us is to blame for past discrimination because we have all inherited this system. Students did not respond directly to my comment.

Joann then found a map online that illustrated how racially segregated the areas surrounding EA continue to be. Dana (white) stated flatly, "I don't agree with that" with no further explanation. When Joann pressed her, she refused to answer. Grace and Emma, both white, left their spots at a table and squeezed over to the couch to be closer to Edward and other white students, creating a physically segregated classroom space.

As the discussion continued, disagreement among students escalated. Finally, after almost a month of near silence, Violet, Juliette, and Lucky began to speak out (Anthony was absent that day).

EMMA: I'm just so sick of this conversation! I'm done with it!

VIOLET: We sit here all year and listen to your history, and the minute we get some of ours, you don't want to hear it! We talked about the Harlem Renaissance for nine days!

Violet's last comment was in response to the many times her white friends had complained, "This is all we ever talk about" regarding class discussions of race. She had expressed a similar reaction to me during our interview, when we talked about the negative response many of her classmates were having toward *The Bluest Eye*. She said:

A lot of people didn't like the Harlem Renaissance either. That . . . was the one actual time that it kind of bothered me, 'cause that's the one thing that's like centered around African American history, and I was like, that one thing, people couldn't stand it. It's like, we talk about your kind all the time, but the one time we get to talk about something that kind of relates to me, you want to have a hissy fit.

More than two months after the fact, Violet admitted to me privately that her friends' negative responses to the Harlem Renaissance unit had bothered her. Yet during that unit she had endured the complaints of the white students patiently, largely without comment.

Class discussion about "The House We Live In" continued:

EMMA: It shouldn't be separated. History is history . . . I don't think it should be called racism. Segregation is not racism. I didn't enslave anybody. I didn't do any of these things or cause inequality. What's happening today is not racism.

Edward and other white students agree with her.

VIOLET, JULIETTE, and LUCKY: Yes it is racism!

They go back and forth this way several times:
   No, it isn't!
   Yes, it is!

JULIETTE: What else would you call it?
LUCKY: If you have people separated by race, it is racism.
EMMA [insisting]: No, it's not racism!
JULIETTE [to Emma]: Why are you so angry?
RON [shaking his spoon at Joann]: Now you're at the point of force-feeding!

Again the discussion erupted into many people talking at once. Dana asked, "What is the point of talking about this? So what if neighborhoods are segregated? Why does it matter?"

In response to Dana's question, I explained that, as a direct result of the policies described in the video, real estate values are still higher in white neighborhoods (Anacker 2010). "Oh," she replied. Two white students, Anna and Tammy, wanted more information about how race affects the housing market. Joann explained that in areas where homes are worth less money, people pay lower taxes, which can affect the services they receive, including education. James asked, "Why would that matter anymore, since people can go to any school they want?" Joann answered that students cannot go to any public school they want; in our area, unless they choose a charter school like EA, they are assigned their public school according to where they live. At that point Ron shifted his anger, calling out, "It's the banks and the government's fault!" He demanded of Joann, "How can we fix this?" Unfortunately, there was no opportunity to answer Ron's question in depth since time had run out and class was over.

Tatum (1997) warns that "poorly organized antiracism workshops or other educational experiences can create a scenario that places participants at risk for getting stuck in their anger" (105). She suggests that whites need to be given concrete tools to help them move beyond guilt and anger and toward antiracist thinking and action. Unfortunately, the hourly starts and stops of secondary school scheduling made it difficult to end classes on a constructive note and may have left students festering in feelings of anger and guilt. I wonder now if a different class structure, perhaps one in which students had been given more opportunity and time to reflect in writing about their feelings, might have been beneficial here.

White Privilege Essay

Joann and I hoped to continue the discussion that had been so intense and had ended so abruptly the next day (and the last of *The Bluest Eye* unit) through analysis of Peggy McIntosh's (2005) seminal essay on white privilege. First published in 1988 but reprinted many times, McIntosh's highly respected and often quoted essay describes white privilege as the unearned, unrecognized advantages that work for whites in large and small ways in everyday life. The most famous and widely used portion of the essay is McIntosh's list of the unearned benefits of whiteness. Students were asked to read and discuss the essay at their tables, and I listened as Lyssa, Edward, Emma, and others read McIntosh's list of privileges aloud, making fun as they read. Lyssa was especially amused by the item, "I can go shopping alone most of the time, pretty well assured that I will not be followed or harassed" (111). Lyssa laughed and said that she had never been followed around in a store. Edward, Emma, and Grace (white students) said they *had* been followed around in stores but believed it was because they are teenagers. Lyssa agreed but then added, "It depends on how they're dressed, like if they look suspicious." The other agreed. Thus, ironically, as these students attempted to refute McIntosh's example of white privilege, the black student in the group claimed she had never been followed, while the white students claimed they had. They all agreed that age, and not race, was the reason that teens might be profiled, but they then shifted their argument to place blame on the way the teens in question might be dressed—they might look "suspicious," in which case this treatment by store personnel would be justified. Significantly, this conversation took place during the height of the Trayvon Martin controversy. Martin, a black teen, was followed in a gated Florida community and, after engaging in a physical conflict, ultimately shot and killed by George Zimmerman, a white Hispanic adult. (More than a year later, Zimmerman was found not guilty of all charges.) Lyssa's argument aligned with those who claimed that Martin's hoodie had made him look suspicious.

As we talked, Anthony wandered over to our table. I filled him in on the conversation, asking if store personnel had ever followed him.

"Tons of times," he shrugged. Then, laughingly, he added, "DeSean Jackson [a professional football player] gets followed around in stores!"

Joann then began the large-group discussion by once again trying to create a "safe space" for students. Echoing Tatum's words from the video she had shown the day before, she stressed, "This is not anybody's fault in this room, it's the world you've inherited. This is hard and controversial to talk about, especially if you think you're being blamed for something that you had nothing to do with." She continued, "So, being aware that we're not to blame, what can we pull out of this article?" As on the previous day, student opinion was divided according to race.

LAURA (white): As AP students, we're taught to look at background. This article was written in 1988, it's outdated in 2012. Number eighteen says, "I can be pretty sure that if I ask to talk to the 'person in charge,' I will be facing a person of my race." We have Obama now.

DANA (white): This article is probably one of the stupidest things I've ever read in my life. This lady sounded completely insane. It's irrelevant today. Maybe a few points are true, but most of them I don't see today.

ANTHONY (African American): That's not fair. She made points that make sense. You might not agree, but it does make sense. She does make some points that are true.

EDWARD (white): It's hard to understand because I keep being told I have privilege. I don't see that, but okay. But I don't understand what I'm supposed to do as a white male. Because there's nothing I can do.

EMMA (white): Besides being a decent human being.

EDWARD: I don't feel I use this advantage. This makes me feel I'm being blamed, but I can't help it.

JOANN: So do you think this problem is unsolvable?

ANTHONY: It takes time, and the gap is getting smaller. It's not fair to blame all white people for what's happening. They were born that way.

JOANN: So how could we have a conversation about race today?

DANA: I don't believe in inequality.

JOANN [ignoring Dana's comment]: How do you talk about racism without white people feeling blamed?

MICHELLE (African American): No one is to blame, but when an institution has been an integral part of society, someone always feels guilty. Racism will always exist because it's such a huge part of society. We can't help hard feelings.

EVIE (white): I personally don't feel to blame. It depends on the person, how you attach your feelings to this.

LUCKY (African American): We're not personally attacking anybody, or the white race overall. But white privilege is dominant.

RON: Only half of these apply.

Ron read aloud from the essay, "I can choose blemish cover or bandages in 'flesh' color that more or less matches my skin" (111), rolling his eyes and laughing. Others joined him. I tried to redirect discussion back to the essay.

MM: But do you see the deeper meaning of this?

JULIETTE [making eye contact with me and nodding]: As African Americans, we're not recognized. Who built this country? If y'all didn't have us, where would y'all be?

JAMES (white): I disagree that it's not as mentioned in the educational system. We spent a whole month on the Harlem Renaissance.

JULIETTE and VIOLET (interrupting forcefully): Oh no! We spent less than nine days on it!

The argument spiraled around in this fashion until Joann, realizing that class time was almost up, asked, "How does it get better?"

As the students stared silently at Joann, I took the opportunity to share some insights from Tatum's (1997) work that I had often used in college classes. Tatum explains that individuals can choose three states of being regarding racism: active racism, passive racism, or antiracism. I explained that people who say blatantly racist things are actively racist, while those who may not initiate racist comments but who go along with them might be considered passively racist. I then explained that, according to Tatum, we can all be antiracist within our own surroundings. "For example," I continued, "not laughing at racist jokes is a way to be antiracist, or serving on a school board or a hiring committee someday, or even voting is a way to be antiracist." As I spoke, I hoped that students would respond positively to the insights I shared, as my own and other white students had done in the past (Flynn 2012).

To my surprise, what I had meant as words of encouragement offended some of my white listeners:

RON: So you're basically saying everyone in this room, except for Laura and a few people, are racist.

JAMES: Almost everyone is passively racist.

MM: But isn't it a matter of choice? The point of this conversation is to raise awareness so that people can choose not to be passively racist.

They shook their heads, insisting that change is impossible because, said Ron, "this is the way we were brought up." Dana agreed, arguing, "This is what we're comfortable with." Although I protested, these white students insisted dismally that no one can measure up to Tatum's (1997) standard of antiracism, and that, for them, change in this direction would be impossible. Violet, who was sitting at their table, looked at me but said nothing.

Students' Written Responses: A More Complete Story

Part of Joann's daily routine with all of her classes involved the use of "Do Nows," brief written exercises that changed each day. Students picked up their Do Now assignments from a plastic tray as they entered the room and were expected to complete them immediately after finding their seats. Joann allowed me the opportunity to write Do Now questions when I was especially interested in students' responses to the literature under study. The Do Nows were collected immediately and entered as part of students' class participation grade; Joann would then give them to me several days or even weeks later among other piles of students' written work. Therefore, I did not usually see the responses students had written until well after the fact.

Near the end of *The Bluest Eye* unit, students completed the following Do Now prompt that I had written: "Take a few minutes to think
about the themes of oppression or marginalization in *The Bluest Eye*. Did
your ideas about race or racism change in any way through the reading of
this book?" Some responses were closely in line with what students had
expressed during class discussions, but others surprised me: I discovered
that several white students who had not voiced their opinions during
group discussions had appreciated and learned from the themes of the
Morrison text.

The majority of students in the class, both white and students of color,
stated that their ideas about racism had not changed through reading Morrison's novel. This, in itself, is not surprising; Naidoo (1992) notes the possibility that antiracist pedagogy "is likely to have a positive effect only on
those who are already more open-minded, and likely to deepen the negative reactions of those with already closed minds" (139). While I believe
that all of the students in 11 Honors would consider themselves to be non-
racists, as I have shown, the responses of some during class discussions illustrated a lack of understanding of the deep and lasting wounds that racism
has inflicted on individuals and on society. Students who had been among
the most vocal and consistent regarding their dislike of the unit reiterated
their feelings in their Do Now responses.[3] James, Emma, Lyssa, and Dana
were among these:

JAMES: No, I still do not believe that racism is a prevalent/common issue, especially in our school. I feel throughout this book I was spoon-fed liberal nonsense that targets white males as the source of the world's problems.

EMMA: Nope.

LYSSA: No; my ideas on race and racism have NOT changed.

DANA: NO.

Again, it is important to stress that I believe these students' presuppo-
sitions were that they were always against racism and so felt no need to
change their views. Their responses do show, however, that they were not
open to deepening their understandings of racism. James's response echoes
the sentiments that he and his close friend, Ron, had shared quite vocally
throughout the unit, and that Ron had represented physically by the spoon
he wore around his neck for the remainder of the school year (with which
he was "spoon-fed liberal nonsense"). James specifically states his belief

that books like *The Bluest Eye* are purposely used to make white males like himself feel unjustly accused of racism. Lyssa and Dana's deliberate use of caps show their frustration with the topic, as does Emma's use of slang and the brevity of her response (while the assignment did not specifically state that students should give more than a one-word answer, these honors students understood that Do Now questions were meant to illicit some degree of reflection).

Along with Lyssa, other African Americans in the class stated that their study of *The Bluest Eye* had not changed their views about race and racism, but the content of their responses, recorded here with no grammatical edits, showed deeper reflection:

KARLA: The way I thought of racism didn't change [because of] the book, it just kind of laid out how people deal with it. Like how people would react to seeing black girls and how they're portrayed/perceived. In a way it made me think of not judging people so quickly because it could have a bigger effect on people then necessary. But nothing really about race.

VIOLET: No my ideas of race did not change after reading 'The Bluest Eye.' I was already exposed to racism and things like that, that happened during that time period.

MICHELLE: Not really. I have always had a wide range of knowledge on racism, so nothing in the novel inspired me to change my ideas on the subject.

LUCKY: No but it make me think of the way racism exist without even existing.

Like the students mentioned above, Violet and Michelle note that their views regarding racism remained unchanged through the reading of *The Bluest Eye*. However, in their responses they took the time to explain that they had thought about racism in the past. Michelle usually agreed with white students during class discussions or remained silent; however, this written response and her comment during discussion of the McIntosh essay—"Racism will always exist because it's such a huge part of society"—show that she did not align herself completely with the opinion of her white friends.

Lucky's response, "No but it make me think of the way racism exist without even existing" indicated that his understandings of racism were deepened through the reading of the novel in that he was challenged to think about the many hidden ways that racism still exists. Perhaps this explains why on a few different occasions Lucky stated he'd never been exposed to racism, but he later named specific incidences through which he or others he knew were targeted by it. Lucky seemed to be actively constructing a deeper understanding of racism and of its impact on him as an African American male (i.e., how racism "exist without even existing") as he progressed through *The Bluest Eye* unit.

Of this group, Karla's answer to the Do Now question was most puzzling to me. Her reflection related directly to the unit's emphasis on the damaging effects of white beauty standards. Karla's quiet personality made it difficult to ascertain if her silence during class discussions was indicative of anything other than her individual temperament, but as one of the dark-skinned African American girls in the class, she did comment that the themes explored in the video *A Girl Like Me* were "true." Interestingly, in her Do Now response, rather than identify with dark-skinned females, Karla took an impersonal approach. While I cannot know for sure, I wonder if this was Karla's way of distancing herself from the painful experience of being one of the "people" who are judged "so quickly" because of physical appearance. What puzzled me most about Karla's answer was her last statement, "But nothing really about race." Did Karla not consider judgmental attitudes toward black girls to be a form of racism, or did she mean that her factual understanding of racism did not change through the reading of this novel? Unfortunately, Karla did not agree to an interview, so I had no opportunity to explore her ideas in depth.

White students who had not spoken out during group discussions wrote the most surprising Do Now responses. Their silence and, in some cases, their close friendships with white students who had expressed resentment and anger during the unit had led me to believe, falsely, that they agreed with these friends. As I read these privately written responses I saw how wrong I had been:

ANNA: My ideas about racism didn't change, but I saw how people were actually effected by it. Also it made racism seem more real than it seems in History class and places like that.

HARRY: The discussions/activities we have done have changed my views. I can see how much more racism goes on in the world secretly through media.

EVIE: Yes because it makes you realize just how deep racism can actually go, intentional or otherwise.

STEPHANIE: Slightly. It surprised me as to how racism still effects people today, it surprised me as to how much it does effect people still/the extent.

Most surprising to me was Ruthie's response. Because of her close friendship with Edward, I had assumed that Ruthie shared his views and possibly even his frustration. But when given the opportunity to express her opinion privately, Ruthie wrote: "After reading this book I realized that racism can be found every where and even unintentional racism still exists and is an issue."

These responses show that some students' understandings of the damaging and continuing effects of racism had been challenged or broadened through their participation in the unit on *The Bluest Eye*. As Anna stated, Morrison's novel made racism seem more real than what she had learned in previous history classes. Yet these white students never expressed their views during the small or large group class discussions when intolerant comments prevailed (Beach, Thein, and Parks 2008; Naidoo 1992). However, based on their written responses, it is safe to say that the silence of these white students did not represent tacit agreement with those who reacted to the Morrison text with anger or resentment.

Laura, one of the white students who had most vehemently defended Walt Whitman against the perceived accusation of racism in the previous chapter, also showed that her understanding of race had been challenged during the weeks we spent on *The Bluest Eye*. She wrote:

> While reading the *Bluest Eye*, my ideas and feelings about race did not change at all. I still feel the same, sad way about racism and how it's utterly stupid and foolish . . . to think any different of someone because they're different from you. I've always felt this way. Actually, reading this book and having these same, circular discussions daily has pointed out differences and race to me when before, I was happily oblivious. Before, I was happily getting along with anyone. Now, I notice color differences and, in all actuality, it bothers me that all of this was pointed out to me, because now I cannot get that annoying back thought out of my head that I'm different. I used to believe that we were all the same. I still want to, but now I feel that I can't.

On the surface, Laura resisted acknowledging present racism and white privilege; a few days after she wrote this response, she argued that the McIntosh (2005) essay was outdated and invalid. However, this written response signifies an important development in Laura's racial identity. Although she states that she has always been against racism, Laura preferred to think that everyone was the same. Now, however, reading and "circular" class discussions of the Morrison novel had caused Laura to question this colorblind approach, through which she had been "happily oblivious" about racial differences. Laura was beginning to denormalize whiteness: she complained that she could not "get it out of her head" that she herself is "different." These feelings created a sense of anxiety in Laura that often accompanies the dissonance whites experience when first challenged with more profound understandings of racism and of their own position of privilege (Helms 1990; Tatum 1997). As uncomfortable as these feelings may be for Laura, they represent a crucial step in developing a more complete understanding of the role of race in her life and in the lives of her African American friends.

Therefore, unbeknownst to me, several white students who had either remained silent throughout class discussions or who, as in the case of Laura, seemed to resist the antiracist ideas that Joann and I presented showed through these written responses that *The Bluest Eye* unit had, in fact, been meaningful to them. Further, students' written responses, recorded within the first few minutes of one particular class, illustrate the complexity and diversity of thinking that students were engaged in during the unit. Such complex student responses require analysis that is equally complex.

From Anger to Helplessness

Although localized and contextualized, the angry and resistant responses of some white students in 11 Honors were not surprising. Many researchers have documented use of similar discourses by whites (Bonilla-Silva 2006; Bush 2004; Gillborn 2009; Leonardo 2002; Marx 2006; McIntyre 1997; Perry 2002; Trainor 2008.) What is somewhat unique, however, is that at EA these responses took place within the context of warm and consistent friendships among students. The finding that cross-racial friendships are less likely to be long-lasting (Rude and Herda 2010) did not seem to hold true at EA, where everyone agreed that long-term cross-racial friendships flourished. As Anthony said, "a lot of people have been here for a long time . . . I mean . . . we know each other."

Long-term cross-racial friendships such as those Anthony described have been found to have positive effects among students of various ages. White students in racially diverse schools who sustained cross-race friendships over time showed greater racial sensitivity and were less likely to excuse racial exclusion with the use of stereotypes. These students were also more apt to describe race-based exclusion as wrong (Killen et al. 2010). Racially biased college students who expressed apprehension about race relations showed a decrease in anxiety when they engaged in cross-racial friendships (Page-Gould, Mendozo-Denton, and Tropp 2008). In light of the benefits of cross-racial friendship, one might have expected the white students in 11 Honors to show greater understanding of the perspectives of their African American friends. And, in fact, if I were to use similar measures of racial understanding as were used in the studies mentioned above, white eleventh graders would have scored well. In class discussions they stated that racial stereotyping and exclusion were wrong, and they showed no anxiety regarding their proximity to students of color; on the contrary, they counted these students as friends. Yet many of them seemed unaware of how their statements would be perceived by these friends. They harshly criticized and even made fun of serious works such as *The Bluest Eye* and the McIntosh (2005) white privilege essay.

Exposure to dominant neoliberal ideology that minimizes the effects of racism may explain white students' overall attitudes about race, but it does not explain the persistence with which they ignored their African American friends' perspectives. There are several possible explanations for the resistive and sometimes insensitive behavior of white students in the eleventh grade honors class. Using Derrick Bell's (2009) theory of interest conversion, one might simply posit that, like many whites, Ron, James, and others will only adopt antiracist positions when it is in their own best interests to do so. These students believed in equal rights for people of color and had a social-emotional stake in maintaining nonracist identities. However, like the whites that Bell describes, they could not accept the idea that "true equality for blacks will require the surrender of racism-granted privileges for whites" (75). According to Bell, it is crucial for whites who wish to give up racial dominance to acknowledge the benefits of whiteness within a continuing system of racism. White students who were not willing to do so employed a variety of discourses, some standard and others contextualized, to avoid conversations about race that might challenge their belief in a "post-racial" society and, therefore, their position of dominance. These students refused to recognize structural racism to avoid admitting that they benefit from these structures. Their friendships with African Americans allowed their nonracist self-concepts to coexist with their angry, insensitive responses about racism. As long as their nonracist stance benefited these students—that is, boosted their self-esteem and heightened their estimation in the eyes of their peers and teachers—Ron, Emma, and the others were strong in their condemnation of racism. But when class discussion required too much focus on the damage of past racism and on the benefits whites derive from living in a present racist system, they grew angry and resisted.

While interest convergence may shed light on students' impulsive refusal to admit their position of dominance, students' responses also indicated the complex emotional spaces they inhabited as they spoke. For example, white students may resist talking about race "out of a genuine desire to see racial equality in the world—a wish that things were more just" (Flynn 2012, 105). For some students the claim that racism is over reflects their desire for it to *be* over (Beach, Thein, and Parks 2008). Perhaps Edward, for example, employed racial evasion, a strategy that "holds that eliminating talk about race will eliminate racism" (Bucholtz 2011, 169), out of a sincere desire to see racism eliminated once and for all. Leah, a Chinese American student, had similar feelings. She wrote in her Do Now response, "I think the best way to stop racism is to stop distinguishing between the 'races.'" Dana's pronouncement, "I don't believe in inequality," which was passed over too quickly to unpack, may sound like a blatant denial of present-day racism but within the context of her friendships with black students might also be interpreted to mean that she doesn't accept inequality, as in, *I don't believe in treating people unequally.*

The emotional dejection, bordering on fatalism, with which students responded to my pep talk on antiracism showed that they cared about racism but felt powerless to effect real change, even within themselves. Cathy, one of the main proponents of the "this is all we ever talk about" discourse, expressed this sense of fatalism in her response to the Do Now question that asked if her views on racism had changed: "No not at all. If anything they reinforced my views & ideas of racism. It will always be prevalent or apparent in our society, no matter how far we come. Humans, by nature, are a judgmental and hateful species." Likewise, Edward's statement, made a few days later during a large group discussion—"I don't understand what I'm supposed to do as a white male. Because there's nothing I can do"— shows the helplessness he feels about racism. Since Edward feels there's nothing he can do about his position of privilege, he feels unjustly blamed for something over which he has no control ("I don't feel I use this advantage. This makes me feel I'm being blamed, but I can't help it"). Ron's shifting of anger toward the government and banks, along with his demand to be told how to fix the problem, show that he did care about the forms of racism described in the California Newsreel (2003) video but felt frustrated and helpless to do anything about them. Ron's and James's belief that "almost everyone is passively racist" could be read as a refusal to change or could signify a discouraged realization that racism does, in fact, exist. The latter indicates an important first step in adopting an antiracist outlook since one cannot begin to move toward antiracist action until one recognizes that racism is a problem.

Along with feeling helpless, white students in 11 Honors experienced feelings of blame when presented with the idea of white privilege. During our interview, Anthony explained his white classmates' resistance to acknowledging racism by stating diplomatically, "I don't wanna say it's guilt, but it's kind of like that." Perhaps partly because of their friendships with black students, these white students had incorporated a "nonracist" identity. It is not surprising that they had difficulty reconciling this identity with the new information about racism and white privilege that Joann and I presented to them, and perhaps explains why some were so dejected at the idea that they might be passively racist (Tatum 1997). As tenth grader B.K. said, "You don't want people to think you're racist. It's just not how you want to be seen or viewed." Helms (1990) argues that the feelings of guilt, helplessness, and anger whites may experience when first faced with the reality of racism are products of the cognitive dissonance that is a necessary step leading to a redefinition of white identity. From this perspective, students' honest responses indicate movement toward deeper reflection about race that may eventually result in a clearer antiracist stance.

Consequently, while white students employed discourses, sometimes quite creatively, to resist the acknowledgment of present-day racism and to mitigate the role of white privilege in their lives, their reasons for doing so were informed by a complicated mix of denial, guilt, and wishful thinking. Long-lasting friendships with students of color complicated white students' responses because through these friendship students had formed comfortable nonracist identities that were challenged by course materials and discussions on race. That being the case, students' angry responses reflected the uncomfortable nature of the identity work that was triggered through their reading and discussion of multicultural literature and accompanying material.

Thinking about Silence

Katherine Schultz (2008) notes, "students' silences can have a range of meanings" (217), and it is likely that students in the eleventh grade honors class were silent during class discussions of *The Bluest Eye* for varied and complex reasons. Certainly, student silences may indicate a trend toward conformity that is not uncommon among adolescents (Lashbrook 2000). Freed from the social risk of disagreeing with their more vocal friends, students who had been silent during class discussions expressed their opposing opinions in their Do Now responses. However, adolescent conformity alone cannot explain the complicated way that silence operated at EA, or how students used silence to express aspects of their racial identities.

Lisa A. Mazzei (2011) explores the role of desire in white silences regarding race. She posits that, for whites, silence satisfies the desire to maintain the status quo because through silence whites avoid being challenged and whiteness remains the unspoken norm. In a sense, all of the white students in 11 Honors used either real or conceptual silence to maintain racial power. The nonparticipating white students used their silence to avoid the uncomfortable challenge that discussions about race might have produced for them. At the same time, the vocal white students demanded silence about race, evidenced through their "Why do we have to keep talking about this?" complaints. The more we talked about racism, the louder their demand for silence became. Both courses of action, while enacted differently, attempted to use silence to achieve the goal of circumventing uncomfortable conversations about racism and white dominance.

Schultz (2009) suggests a different way that students may use silence as a tool. For some, silence in the classroom may be a way to reject domination by the more vocal students. She explains, students may "resist verbal participation because the possibility for speech or contributions to a discussion appear too limiting. If only certain discourses are allowed, it may not be worth speaking" (31). In this case, silence does not indicate agreement but may suggest just the opposite. The silence of students from varied racial backgrounds in 11 Honors may have been a method of active resistance to the dominating voices of Emma, Ron, and the other white students whose complaints about discussions of racism overtook the class dynamic.

The patience and restraint of the African American students who did finally speak out during the last few classes of *The Bluest Eye* unit reflect the complicated processes at work in them as they positioned themselves on the topic of racism in relation to their white friends. Like the white students who remained silent during group discussion, African American students may have used silence to resist the dominating voices in the class. However, it is also conceivable that Violet, Anthony, and the others used silence to protect themselves from the hurt of witnessing their white friends' insensitivity and resentment (Beach, Thein, and Parks, 2008). Schultz (2009) describes this response in a Mexican American student, Luis, who she believes used classroom silence "as a self-protective refusal to engage in the complicated racial and cultural dynamics of the classroom" (34).

In order to discover the multiple meaning of silence in the classroom, Schultz (2009) suggests that teachers take an "inquiry stance toward silence" (121); in other words, teachers and students should collaborate to investigate the role of silence in the classroom. While Joann and I did not address students' silences with the class as a whole, during our interview I did ask Anthony why he and the other African American students were so quiet during most of the class discussions about racism. Anthony's response was enlightening. He explained:

> I think, one, because we don't want to make people feel bad. I know that's one big thing. Like we don't want to, you know, blame everything on, like, because we, in this school, particularly, we've been, a lot of people have been here . . . for a long time . . . we know each other. We're not trying to blame each other for, you know, like, something like that . . . it's a touchy-feely subject. You don't want to blame your friends for some things like racism.

Gilda L. Ochoa and Daniela Pineda (2008) propose a general explanation for patterns of interaction among students such as the one that developed in 11 Honors. They found that, ironically, during a course on diversity, student participation patterns replicated the same power dynamic that the course material was meant to critique. Because, through classroom behaviors, students will tend to reproduce the racially constructed social positioning they have experienced in life, black and Hispanic students felt uncomfortable and restricted in the presence of white students who offered their opinions more forcefully. Therefore, as was the case in 11 Honors, white students dominated discussions while students of color remained largely silent. Through their participation patterns, students replicated the socio-racial roles they'd been surrounded by throughout their lives.

Anthony's explanation made me wonder if societal behavioral patterns among races might be functioning in an even more specific way during *The Bluest Eye* unit. I wondered if he and other black students were fulfilling a deeply ingrained societal role that Toni Morrison explores in *Playing in the Dark* (1993), a work of literary criticism. Morrison examines the character of Jim in Mark Twain's *The Adventures of Huckleberry Finn* ([1884] 1996), the "unassertive, loving, irrational, passionate, dependent, inarticulate" (57) slave whose function in the novel is to serve the white children, Huck and Tom, at the expense of his own freedom and dignity. Anthony explained that he and other African American students in the class disagreed with their white friends but for the greater part of the unit kept silent in order to spare their friends' feelings. They were, Anthony said, "holding their tongues" in order to protect their white friends from feeling blamed for racism, and when they did speak out, they were careful to absolve their white friends from personal responsibility for racism. One might argue that the loyalty black students felt for their white friends put them at risk of adopting a subordinate position in the dynamics of the classroom. In the same way that, as Morrison describes, black characters in literature often function to service white characters, African American students in 11 Honors suppressed their own voices in order to protect the feelings of their white friends.

Thus, through their patient silence, African American students inadvertently created the "safe space" for their white friends that Joann believed to be so important. Perhaps the patience the African American eleventh graders displayed during class discussions indicates their self-confidence and strong sense of identity (Matrenec 2011). However, I worry that the dynamic that existed among these students, partly informed by their cross-racial friendships, ultimately reproduced the white hegemony that has existed for centuries past, wherein the role of African Americans is to service the needs of the whites around them.

Close relationships with whites may have informed African American students' silences on another level, as well. Ravi Hansra Matrenec (2011) found that African American males who attended a mostly white suburban school felt that they had "something to prove" (231) to the white students and teachers that surrounded them. In order to combat racist stereotypes, black males who had grown up in the suburban context of the school felt they needed to behave well and not associate with the more newly arrived black students who got into fights and showed other disruptive behaviors.

Matrenec explains that in "a reverse of self-fulfilling prophecy" (231), these students felt they needed to prove to others and to themselves that they did not meet the stereotypical image of the trouble-making, underachieving African American male. Similarly, Karolyn Tyson (2011) describes the difficult social situation that African American students in higher academically tracked classes like 11 Honors may experience. She found that because of their underrepresentation in higher-level classes, these students dissociated themselves from other black students they deemed "loud and ghetto" (57). Thus, African American students who attend white-dominated classes may feel compelled to take sides against other African American students whose behaviors whites find unacceptable. Ochoa and Pineda (2008), too, found that students of color felt pressured to counter white stereotypical beliefs about them through their behavior. With the same "double consciousness" that W.E.B. Du Bois ([1903] 2005) described in 1903, black students who attend white-dominated schools or classes may experience a "sense of always looking at one's self through the eyes of others" (7). Anthony's, Lucky's, Juliette's, Karla's, and Violet's silence may partly be explained by their double consciousness; they were aware of how their opinions would be perceived by their white friends and classmates. Violet's "I'm black and I'm proud" assurance, given in response to Ron's insensitive remarks, illustrates the pressure she and other African Americans experience in "measuring one's soul by the tape of a world that looks on in amused contempt and pity" (Du Bois [1903] 2005, 7).

African American honors students who had been at EA for several years were invested in their relationships with their white peers and were careful to present calm, reasonable personas that would not provoke fear or discomfort in whites. It was clear, however, that Juliette and Violet cared deeply about unpacking racism in class: one day, after listening quietly to their white classmates complain that race "is all we ever talk about," the two girls approached Joann privately and thanked her for including racism in the curriculum. "We got your back," they told her. Although the girls may have felt cautious about opposing their friends' ideas openly, they appreciated Joann's willingness to deal with a topic that they felt was important and relevant.

It is important to note that eventually Anthony, Violet, Juliette, and Lucky did speak out in disagreement with their white friends; their choice to wait until the end of the unit might be seen as an exercise in power. Schultz (2009) notes, "Whether intended or not, holding on to silence before speaking often allows a person to be heard" (38). Rather than refuting the comments of white students who spoke against the salience of racism at every turn, these African American students listened patiently. Toward the end of the unit, when they were ready, they spoke up collaboratively and forcefully, perhaps finding strength in their careful choice of words. The silence of Violet, Anthony, and others may have ensured that when they did finally speak, they would be heard. In this respect, teachers may understand silence not as an absence, but as a strategy that will prepare the environment for communication when silent students do choose to speak (Schultz 2009).

"How Can We Fix This?"

Ron's question, asked in frustration, was an important one that can be applied broadly to the findings of this study. A school like EA, more racially diverse than many suburban high schools, provides opportunity for students to form long-lasting cross-racial friendships that, given the segregated nature of many suburban neighborhoods, students may not otherwise have opportunity to form. Students at this school will, in one sense, be prepared to enter diverse college and career environments without the anxiety that young people who did not mix with peers of diverse backgrounds expressed (Page-Gould, Mendozo-Denton, and Tropp 2008). However, this study has shown that conviviality does not necessarily indicate the absence of racial tensions in a high school setting. While of course there are no easy fixes, my concluding chapter explores some possible approaches to help students and teachers grapple with an often difficult subject in a way that fosters understanding of all perspectives.

Conclusion

■ ■ ■ ■ ■ ■ ■ ■ ■ ■ ■ ■ ■ ■ ■ ■

"How Can We Fix This?"

Decades have passed since Derrick Bell, Gloria Ladson-Billings, and others established the foundational concepts of critical race theory, and since then many studies have examined students' ideas about race and their behaviors as racialized beings. The list of scholars stressing the importance of students engaging directly with race and urging schools to rethink practices entrenched in institutional racism continues to grow. Despite the insights gained through scholarly examination of the role of race in education, little has changed about the way race functions in schools like Excellence Academy. Race is still not often discussed, and many teachers and administrators adopt the "heroes and holidays" approach to multicultural education, ignoring the role of race in maintaining power hierarchies. In many classrooms, racism is presented as a historical phenomenon with little connection to students' everyday lives.

While the close cross-racial friendships and lack of racial antagonism at EA do represent progress in a general sense, this study has shown that cross-racial friendships alone do not guarantee that youth are incorporating antiracist understandings into their racial identities. In fact, those same friendships may produce unexpected consequences, such as when the outwardly friendly environment at EA made the frustration and feelings of marginalization many students and faculty experienced less visible, encouraged student silences, and allowed for administrative decisions that limited educational opportunities for all students. Through the following discussion I hope to suggest ways that schools like Excellence Academy can look beyond their congenial environment to examine practices that hinder antiracist pedagogy and limit students' understandings of race relations.

Institutional Practices

When students are immersed in a school culture that does not recognize the challenges faced by those outside the dominant group, it is not reasonable to expect students to understand or appreciate those challenges. If schools are to engage students in critical thinking regarding racism, they must take into account how their own institutional processes work against students' incorporation of antiracist understandings.

The Ethos of Excellence

Jennifer Seibel Trainor (2008) suggests that discussions of systemic white privilege will do little to impact racist beliefs in white students if the school's "emotioned rules" (12) tacitly help to perpetuate these beliefs. She found that while reading Maya Angelou's (1969) *I Know Why the Caged Bird Sings*, white students categorized Angelou as "a whiner" (90) for her depictions of racism in the text. Trainor argues that school slogans, posters, and other such motivational exhortations to "focus on the positive" (90) strengthened the inclination in white students to believe that black authors, like Angelou, who wrote about their experiences with racism were whining or complaining. In the students' view, shouldn't Angelou be expected to focus on the positive in relating her life story? Similarly, Amanda Lewis (2006) found that belief in American meritocracy was deeply imbedded in school culture at a white-dominated school and, therefore, used by students to explain economic disparities. Students attributed wealth and poverty to people's hard work or laziness.

While it is commendable that teachers and administrators at EA worked hard to promote an ethos of academic excellence, an overdependence on neoliberal notions of individualism and meritocracy may have inadvertently reinforced students' belief that people who suffer under oppression should simply "stop whining" and do something about their oppressed state. In fact, Joann's students were warned against whining through the following "classroom norm," displayed on a poster: "Remember that *academics* are *your current job*: whining, complaining, and arguing are inappropriate and unprofessional."

Joann's "Classroom Norms"

1. *Be prepared* with ALL necessary materials at the start of the class.
2. Begin your *Do Now* as soon as you enter the classroom.
3. Recognize that *class time* is for *class work*.
4. Follow the *Dress Code* and *Code of Conduct* at all times.
5. Demonstrate *respect* (including body language and eye contact) when others are speaking.
6. Wait until an *appropriate* transition to go to the bathroom, ask a question, or get something.
7. Use *formal conventions* for ALL oral and written responses.
8. Remember that *academics* are *your current job*: whining, complaining, and arguing are inappropriate and unprofessional.

Teachers reinforced the idea that "complaining" is unprofessional and childish through personal interactions with students as well. For example, when eleventh grader Jack complained to Megan (an administrator) that he could not focus on an in-class assignment because students seated near him were talking and singing, she told him, "You need to ask the adults at your table to stop talking." "What adults?" Jack asked incredulously. "They're all talking! They're acting like five-year-olds!" In spite of Jack's protests, Megan did not intervene. The noise level increased, and Jack became involved in a heated exchange with a female student that disrupted the writing activity further until they both finally trailed off into frustrated silence. It is conceivable that interactions such as this, added to the "classroom norms" posted on Joann's wall, helped inform students' belief that oppressed characters in literature were themselves at fault for not taking action. If students were expected to be fully responsible for their success, why weren't others held up to that same standard of behavior? This may explain why many eleventh graders showed impatience with Hester Prynne, the oppressed female protagonist of Nathaniel Hawthorne's *The Scarlet Letter*. Students referred to Hester as "stupid" and "passive," and didn't understand "why she didn't just leave." Thus, as Trainor (2008) and

Lewis (2006) found, the hidden curriculum of individual responsibility may have informed a racial identity in some students that did not encourage understanding or empathy for people who were not part of the privileged, dominant group and who had suffered at the hands of that group.

The ethos of excellence at EA was also responsible for the "classroom norm" that outlawed all but "formal conventions" of language in Joann's classes. As noted, strict adherence to such policies normalizes whiteness and acts as a symbolic boundary (Carter 2012) to maintain insider status for whites and outsider status for those whose language practices differ from this "norm." For some students, low academic achievement may reflect their feelings of outsider status (Carter 2005). While, as Lisa Delpit (2004) explains, direct instruction in speech, grammar, and writing style is a necessary component of academic success for most children, students should also be taught to think critically about the power structures that make using certain dialects unacceptable in formal settings. As an alternative to outlawing students' home language practices in the classroom, Ladson-Billings (2009) suggests that teachers employ culturally relevant pedagogy: that is, pedagogy that challenges students to excel academically while empowering them "intellectually, socially, emotionally, and politically" (20). Culturally relevant teaching helps students make connections between academic content and their home contexts, and requires teachers to support students of all cultural and language backgrounds (Durden and Truscott 2013). Students' home dialects, language practices, and communication styles can be affirmed and welcomed into the classroom even as students are equipped with the reading, writing, and speaking skills they will need to succeed in their future academic and career endeavors. If teachers are given the proper tools and training, schools like EA do not need to give up their goal of academic excellence in order to create an environment where all students feel a sense of belonging.

The Prevalence of Uncritical Multiculturalism

The administration at EA may have attempted to foster a sense of belonging for African American students through the schools' recognition of Black History Month, but shallow, tokenistic celebrations are no substitute for critical examination of important social issues. The persistence of uncritical forms of multiculturalism in education supports students' constructions of race as cultural difference that has little connection to past and present injustices or to their daily lives. Through its focus on "celebrating differences," uncritical multiculturalism essentializes cultural characteristics and may reinforce rather than dispel stereotypes. Further, by failing to examine systemic inequity, curriculum steeped in uncritical multiculturalism implies that race is no longer a stratifying societal force (Sleeter 2005).

Edward W. Said (1979) famously coined the term *Orientalism* to describe the Western construction of knowledge about the Middle East (aka "the Orient") that positioned the West as the dominating standard of normalcy and the Middle East as the exotic, inferior "other." Schools and classrooms that "celebrate diversity" through an uncritical approach to multicultural content ignore social inequities and, in a modern version of Said's Orientalism, focus instead on difference through cultural customs. Uncritical multiculturalism normalizes whiteness and places students of color in the position of "other": the exotic "minorities" whose racial or ethnic backgrounds place them outside the norm of the majority culture. For this reason, uncritical focus on cultural diversity may work as a potential tool of interest convergence. While recognizing multiculturalism appears to be the opposite of colorblind practice, celebratory recognitions of cultural diversity can reinforce whites' view of self as being devoid of race or culture and can encourage whites to think of culture as an exotic commodity owned by other people (Salter and Adams 2013). Whites benefit from this approach because as long as they themselves remain raceless, they can ignore the ways they continue to benefit from racism. Therefore, through engaging in practices related to uncritical multiculturalism, whites are able to maintain the façade of antiracism without the fear of losing dominant status.

The administrative decision at EA to celebrate Black History Month through a performance by the (white) West African dance troupe is an example of uncritical multiculturalism that positions race as an exotic quality to be "celebrated" and not as a socially constructed hierarchal system that has advantaged whites and oppressed people of color for centuries. Schools and classrooms that adopt this approach fail to explore in any depth the realities of class struggle, poverty, and disenfranchisement experienced by groups outside of the white, middle-class experience. Instead, through uncritical multiculturalism, teachers and administrators present students with the easy fix of recognizing cultural differences as the key to positive race relations (McCarthy and Dimitriadis 2005). Through add-on multicultural celebrations such as the West African dance event, teachers and administrators perpetuate the idea that appreciating cultural difference is all that is needed to achieve racial equity (May and Sleeter 2010).

Attempts at uncritical multiculturalism did not only originate with the administration at EA; students, too, tried to incorporate multiculturalism into their school program through the formation of the "cultural foods club" that met once a month during lunch period in Joann's classroom. The club organizers were the female "artsy nerds" I describe in previous chapters, and the purpose of the club was simply to eat "ethnic" foods, provided by club members. While I enjoyed the pizza, tortilla chips, and salsa that appeared during these sessions as much as everyone else, as Sonia Nieto (2005) points out, "multicultural education without an explicit antiracist focus may perpetuate the worst kinds of stereotypes if it focuses only on superficial aspects of culture and the addition of ethnic tidbits to the curriculum" (405). The defining of ethnic difference through food consumption by students at EA seemed an apt reflection of how multiculturalism had been presented to them throughout their educational experience. I add my voice to the chorus of researchers and advocates who insist that multicultural school curriculum should focus on helping students to think critically about race and not on tokenistic celebrations, events, or activities. Teachers and the curriculum they choose must engage students in critical multiculturalism, which addresses specific issues of power, privilege, and structural inequity based not only on race but also on social class, gender, sexuality, religion, and other relevant factors.

Academic Tracking and Racial Identity

While tokenistic multicultural celebrations exoticize the cultural backgrounds of some students and normalize those of others, academic tracking practices have the potential to influence students' racial identities in even more profound ways. Meant to improve instruction through homogeneous ability grouping, academic tracking often creates de facto racial segregation in racially diverse schools like EA, with African American and Latino/a students populating the low-track classes in disproportionate numbers (Dickens 1996; Oakes 2005; Tyson 2011). Because of academic tracking, desegregation does not necessarily guarantee integration (Carter 2012; Perry 2002; Tyson 2011; Welton 2013). As honors student Anthony explained, "in our school in general, most of the white kids are in excelled classes and most of the black kids are in unexcelled classes, so there's not much time for each other to get to know each other."

Mixed-race classrooms can potentially provide "contact zones" for students, described by Mary Louise Pratt (1998) as "social spaces where cultures meet, clash, and grapple with each other, often in contexts of highly asymmetrical relations of power" (173). The racial segregation caused by academic tracking makes such encounters impossible and prevents students of diverse racial backgrounds from hearing each other's perspectives (Kubitschek and Hallinan 1998; Luther 2009; Stoughton and Sivertson 2005). While the class discussions about race that took place at EA were difficult and even painful for some students, the fact is that these conversations did take place, and students were eventually able to hear perspectives and opinions that differed from their own. I cannot help but wonder how the presence of African American students from the eleventh grade on-level class, students like Daniel, Samar, and Rihanna, might have enhanced and deepened discussions surrounding *The Bluest Eye*. Carter (2012) argues that academic tracking promotes cultural meanings that "neutralize the effects of resourceful schools as a conduit for equal educational opportunities" (161). Tragically, academic tracking practices limited the educational experience of all eleventh graders at EA.

The educational limitations caused by tracking are closely related to the way such practices influence student identity as well. Carter (2012) explains that students and teachers make meanings of the way certain groups tend to dominate in specific settings. She notes that "various school settings acquire meanings as the specific 'turfs' of one group or another. That is, an implicit belief emerges that certain individuals or groups belong to a particular academic or extracurricular program" (4). Because schools act as powerful socializing agents, students receive messages about themselves through their daily school experiences. High-tracked students receive the message that they can achieve, and low-tracked students receive the message that they cannot. Hence, students who are academically tracked internalize the legitimacy of an academic pecking order without fully realizing the effect it is having on their identity. Aware of classroom demographics, students naturalize academic achievement as a function of race (Carter 2012; Oakes 2005; Stoughton and Sivertson 2005; Tyson 2011). Tracking puts African American students at within-group social risk as well because higher-achieving black students may feel the need to distance themselves from their lower-achieving counterparts, relying on stereotypes to categorize their peers and describing them as "ghetto" and "loud" (Rosenbloom 2010; Tyson 2011).

I have shown that even though African American students at EA did not accuse their higher-achieving black friends of "acting white" because of their academic success, they did recognize the racial segregation caused by the school's tracking system and believed that race played a part in maintaining the school's academic hierarchy. As eleventh grader Samar said in a moment of frustration, "My skin color stops me from leading." Though some were frustrated by their lack of academic success, students developed a disposition that connected academic placement with race.

More about Understanding Silences

When students of various backgrounds are given opportunity to share the classroom, educators must find ways for all students to express their voices, and must take into account the role and meaning of students' silences in the classroom. Schultz (2008) reminds us that teachers should not make assumptions about students who choose to remain silent during class discussions. White teachers, in particular, may interpret students' silences through a lens of racial supremacy, assuming that white students are silent because of individual style while Asian Americans may be "naturally quiet" and African Americans disengaged. Instead, Schultz recommends that teachers interrogate students' silences and learn from them. Silence in the classroom can tell us much about individual student's responses and can help us to understand the racialized group dynamic of the classroom.

Although I participated in four of Joann's literature classes, student silences were most evident in the 11 Honors class. Generally speaking, this was not a quiet group. As I've mentioned, due to the close friendships in the class, Joann often felt she had trouble keeping private conversations to a minimum and staying on track during her lessons. Many students entered the room singing, talking, and laughing, and often Joann used her own silence to quiet the group, staring at them motionlessly as she waited for them to notice and settle down. Only a few students in the group, including Harry (white), Leah (Chinese American), and Karla (African American), seemed to be quiet as a function of personality. Of course, there was the occasional student who came to class tired and disengaged, and, as in most classes, intermittent moments of boredom overtook us all. Generally speaking, though, the silences in 11 Honors signified many levels of student response (Schultz 2009), indicated students' complex and often unexamined feelings about race, and reflected the difficult group dynamic that I describe in the previous chapter. I have argued that students used silence to both resist and protect themselves from the dominant classroom discourse that refused to acknowledge the salience of racism. Further, the adolescent trend toward conformity and—for African American students—the desire to protect their white friends from feeling blamed for racism influenced students' silences during class discussions about race.

Silences that followed Joann's sharing of difficult or challenging information may have also indicated that students were processing that information and needed more time to think about issues before responding. The commonly practiced pedagogy wherein teachers ask questions and students are expected to give immediate answers allows little time for deeper thought about important subjects. In retrospect, I believe that our pressing of students to respond verbally and quickly to challenging issues may have added to the lopsided group dynamic that became the pattern of interaction in 11 Honors. Our need for immediate response fed some students' tendencies to answer too quickly, and in so doing exacerbated the insensitive approach they took. Other students may have felt shut down by our attempts to lead group discussions, not feeling comfortable enough to comment on information to which they had only recently been exposed.

When reflective silence is welcomed as a method of participation, it can be a useful tool to stimulate deeper thinking and more careful responses (Schultz 2008). In the following I suggest specific ways that we might have fostered more reflective integration of curricular materials in order to give all students an opportunity to think deeply about the difficult topic of race and, as they felt ready, to share their thoughts with their friends and classmates.

Attending to Students' Writing

Allowing students' more time to write about their thoughts when challenging issues emerge in school curriculum might help to encourage a more thoughtful level of reflection for some students. While students are regularly bombarded with content and analysis questions (often in the form of literature "packets") that they must complete for a classwork grade, rarely are they asked to share their feelings about curriculum in a sustained, private way. In the eleventh grade honors class, the silence of some students opened up space for a group of vocal white students to dominate class discussion with resistant discourse, some of which may have been as much a function of resisting adult authority as resisting ideas about racism and white privilege. Daily student journaling throughout *The Bluest Eye* unit, in particular, may have defused some of this resistance and helped students to move beyond their initial responses and think more deeply about why this unit elicited the feelings or silences in them that it did (Ochoa and Pineda 2008). The journaling process used in classrooms usually does not require students to share their writing with others in the class, but journals may be collected for teacher feedback. Through this method teachers have opportunity to ask probing questions in a private context, and—if the student is willing—a continuous, meaningful conversation between student and teacher will develop. Later on, once students have had time to establish their ideas and work through their feelings, they may be invited (but not forced) to share some of their writings with others in the class or to express their feelings though artistic or other sensory modalities (Schultz 2009).

While my "Do Now" question regarding students' responses to *The Bluest Eye* was a small attempt to use students' writing to access their ideas, the exercise was problematic in both its lack of process and our failure to offer the students feedback on their responses. Ongoing journaling would provide a sustained method of reflection with the benefit of immediate teacher feedback that may help students to process challenging ideas about race.

Incorporating Technology into Pedagogy

Technology may help teachers provide another method for students to communicate their ideas and feelings in a manner that does not privilege the more extroverted members of the class. As I noted in my study of religiously conservative college students' constructions of race (Modica 2012), web platforms that allow students opportunity to post in a discussion board, blog, or wiki format may help generate fruitful conversation among students for a few reasons. First, many students spend hours online outside of school and are comfortable with this venue. Second, students who are not comfortable sharing their opinions in person may find that writing allows them a freedom of expression they haven't experienced during class sessions. Third, when postings are asynchronous (i.e., not synchronous or "live" chats), students have opportunity to read and think about others' postings before responding with their own, and to edit their own comments before posting, perhaps allowing for deeper and more careful reflection. Ironically, EA was initiated several years ago under the charter of technology; use of technology was meant to make the school stand apart from the "regular" district-run public schools in the area. Since then the school has dropped the extended use of technology from its charter, and while students sometimes have access to computers in the classroom, technology is used mainly for research; hence, its potential as an effective participation methodology is greatly underrealized. Since college-level courses often use synchronous and asynchronous discussion to encourage student participation, schools like EA that purport to be college preparatory in nature should think seriously about incorporating technology that would provide students the opportunity to be heard in a variety of formats.

Defining Racism and Privilege

Finding ways to encourage students' participation in conversations about race involves pedagogical considerations on more than one level. While reflective writing and discussion forums may be helpful in circumventing an unbalanced group dynamic, choice of curricular materials is also crucial. Inclusion of texts and supplementary materials that help students define racism as a contemporary and structural social problem is vital to a critical approach to multiculturalism. Whites who tend to view racism as individual prejudice and ignore institutional racism can more easily set aside discrimination as someone else's problem. Academic and economic achievement gaps among groups are then directly attributed to the behavioral successes or failures of individuals within those groups (Greene and Abt-Perkins 2003; Perry 2011), and not to past and present institutional practices that sustain the racialized status quo (Nieto 2005). Teachers and schools who ignore structural racism do not support students in constructing understandings of race relations that are relevant to their time and place (Lewis 2006). The problem at EA was not that students condoned racism; on the contrary, the cross-racial friendships at the school allowed many students to view themselves as progressive in their thinking about race. Rather, the problem was that the prevailing definition of racism as individual prejudice or bias was too narrow. Students resisted Joann's attempts to point out examples of structural racism, instead clinging to a limited definition that enabled them to produce contextualized discourses to avoid discussions of race and to view themselves, as whites, as victims of discrimination.

While teachers may hope that multicultural texts will be effective tools in broadening students' thinking about racism, they must also consider how students' ideas about race will influence their analysis of those texts. Reading texts that explore past oppression is not enough to foster antiracist awareness; the study of multicultural curriculum must offer students the tools to critique past *and* present power systems that work to perpetuate racism (Schultz 2009). Students who view racism as a past social problem that was largely resolved by the civil rights movement will be likely to interpret the texts they read through the lens of that definition.

The responses to *The Bluest Eye* that I describe in this study serve as an important example of how students' understandings of racism influenced, and in some cases limited, the benefit that their teacher hoped they would derive from reading the text. Set before the civil rights movement, the racism that characters experienced was so blatant that students would be hard-pressed to find that degree of racially motivated hatefulness in their everyday lives. Therefore, while condemning the racism in the novel, students could easily dismiss it as the abhorrent behavior of select individuals and as something that no longer exists. Likewise, Joann's use of the *Frontline* "A Class Divided" video, which depicts racist sensibilities from 1968, may have confirmed the idea for students that racism is a thing of the past. Although Joann's inclusion of multicultural texts into her curriculum was meant to broaden students' thinking about race, it also, in some cases, reified students' already limited definition of racism.

Of course, along with examples of individual racism depicted in *The Bluest Eye*, Toni Morrison also explores institutional racism and the privileging of whiteness; her exposé of the damaging effects of whiteness as the standard of beauty is a clear example of racism that reaches far beyond the behavior of individual people. The time setting of the novel, though, again allows students to dismiss Morrison's critique as no longer applicable to the state of race relations today and allows students like Emma to claim, "There's plenty of representation" of people of color in beauty advertisements. Kristin Luther (2009) found a similar response from a white student after reading Harper Lee's (1960) *To Kill a Mockingbird*; while recommending that the text be kept in the curriculum to foster understanding of the past, this student wrote, "'Today's United States, does not have racism and all men are created equal. . . . In modern culture, racism is nearly non-existent'" (214). Carter (2012), too, found that white students objected to discussing racism in class because, as one white student said, "'We're past that . . .'" (134). The belief that racism is no longer a relevant issue is, of course, what fueled the sentiment in Ron and other students at EA that African Americans should "get over" racism. How tragic that these important works of literature meant to expose racism may instead confirm students' beliefs that racism is over since, from students' perspectives, race relations are far improved from the situations depicted in the texts.

The phenomenon of white privilege may also be misunderstood by white students, especially those of working-class backgrounds who do not consider themselves to be privileged (Beach, Thein, and Parks 2008). Students who define privilege as wealth or immediate opportunity may more readily dismiss the idea of white privilege as not applicable to their context. Perry (2002) found a variety of responses from white students regarding white privilege: some used reverse racism arguments to insist that blacks received more privileges than they did while others recognized historic white privilege but argued against its salience in modern life. Similarly, students in all of Joann's classes mentioned affirmative action in job opportunities and scholarships to argue that blacks are now more privileged than whites. Therefore, it is essential to help students explore white privilege as a phenomenon created by past and present structural and individual racism, not as a guarantee that all whites will live privileged lives. As Tatum (1997) explains, "while all Whites benefit from racism, they do not benefit equally" (12). Critical race theorist Cheryl Harris (1993) describes whiteness as a "'consolation prize': it does not mean that all whites will win, but simply that they will not lose, if losing is defined as being at the bottom of the social and economic hierarchy" (1759). Many white students who attend EA live in working-class neighborhoods, and some travel from economically depressed areas in Carltonville. However, because of past racist housing policies that created segregated neighborhoods, white students are more likely to live in the safer section of Carltonville, where property values are higher and where gun violence is not a common occurrence as it is, for example, in Anthony's part of town. Anthony told me that during the previous school year he had lost a friend to gun violence just a block away from his home.

Therefore, using works of historical fiction that depict the cruelty suffered by people of color at the hands of whites may not help white students understand themselves as racialized beings and the recipients of white privilege. Students like Edward and James, who saw themselves as decent people and who were friendly with students of color, related neither to the African Americans in *The Bluest Eye* nor to their white oppressors. If the goal of incorporating multicultural literature into school curriculum is to help students understand their own positioning as entrenched members of a racial hierarchy, educators need to use literature and supplementary materials that more closely depict that position for all students. White students who have not been challenged to think critically about their racial identity and who do not have hostile feelings toward members of other racial groups are likely to have difficulty understanding racism as a prevailing social structure to which they are linked and from which they benefit (Naidoo 1992). In other words, along with important works of historical fiction like *The Bluest Eye* that may help students to understand the experience of past victims of racism, students need to read texts that depict racism in the present and that contain characters to whom all students can relate. White students need to read about antiracist whites who become allies to people of color. The fact that such texts may be hard to locate points out not only the need to expand the canon of multicultural literature currently in use in schools but perhaps even the need for publishers to seek out and encourage authors of such works.

Given students' feelings that fiction is a less-than-reliable account of human experience, teachers might consider incorporating more memoirs like *A Long Way Gone* and *Night* into their curriculum. Almost a year after I had completed my fieldwork, Joann wrote to ask for my help in choosing a contemporary memoir that depicted racism from the perspective of a person of color in the United States, and we had difficulty finding more than a few titles that fit that description. However, while there seems to be a lack of both memoirs and realistic fiction that explore structural racism in a contemporary setting, there is no lack of ethnographies that do the same. Perhaps secondary school educators would do well to add scholarly works of ethnography to their curriculum. Likewise, ethnographers and academic publishers need to view high school students as a viable market for their scholarly works.

Hence, while works of historical fiction are important to help students understand our nation's racist history, teachers also need to adopt methods and curriculum that will intentionally challenge students' ideas about the role of race in their everyday lives. Joann was on the right track with her white beauty standards collage assignment, which encouraged critical exploration of race in media. Her future lessons might also include a wider critique of media sources (movies, television, video games, etc.) and might more intentionally encourage teenagers to reflect on their own experiences with racism. Assignments that deconstruct racism in areas that are relevant to students' lives can help them, in eleventh grader Lucky's words, "think of the way racism exist without even existing." Welcoming students' home worlds into the classroom and encouraging them to partner with community members through interviews and neighborhood observations, for example, will encourage participation and engagement in issues of race and identity that are meaningful to students (Schultz 2009).

Offering Support

My experience at Excellence Academy confirmed something I had known for years: for many people, talking about race in mixed-race settings, even among friends, is difficult. Simply plopping race into the curriculum may be counterproductive unless students and teachers receive support as they engage in conversations about race.

Supportive Confrontation for Students

Innovative pedagogy and more inclusive curricular efforts are crucial elements in creating a school environment that encourages youth to consider the ongoing role race plays in all of our lives. These efforts, though, must be offered in a classroom environment that simultaneously promotes an atmosphere of trust and challenge (Naidoo 1992). Teachers like Joann and me must be willing to partake in a balancing act: we must understand the emotional place our students speak from (Beach, Thein, and Parks 2008; Flynn 2012; Trainor 2008) while at the same time pushing those students to think beyond their comfort zone about race and other important social issues. We must respect the voices of all students, even those with whom we do not agree. However, while respect is essential to any productive discussion, respect without challenge will not lead to broader perspectives for students, and too much emphasis on emotional safety can impede critical analysis of race relations. Alice McIntyre (1997) warns that attempts to maintain a "culture of niceness" (40) can impede genuine critique of white privilege. If students expect to be emotionally comfortable at all times, they may not be prepared for the challenge of discussing racism.

Striking the balance between respect and challenge may, unfortunately, be easier said than done, and students' emotional responses can be dramatic and uncomfortable for all. Zeus Leonardo (2002) describes several incidences when white women answered critiques of whiteness with tears, sometimes disrupting the discussion by leaving the room. Recently, during one of my own college classes, a female student responded in the very same way. The student had suggested her mother as an example of someone who "isn't really racist, but is just older and so thinks a certain way." When I noted kindly, but firmly, that the student's mother was likely younger than I am, and that age is not an excuse for intolerance, the student's eyes welled with tears and she fled into the hallway. Leonardo (2002) explains that through such behavior whites refocus attention from oppressed people to themselves, positioning themselves as victims and winning the sympathies of those around them. Whites who behave in this way shift the group focus to themselves, highlighting their own feelings of discomfort in order to avoid dealing with the difficult subject at hand. Through this incident I experienced the same fear of accusation that I found to be present in teachers at EA. What if this student reported me to the college administration? Would I be able to explain my response in a way that the college's administrators, all of whom are white, would understand? Fortunately, I was able to resolve the issue with the student with no need for administrative involvement, but I must admit that the incident did cause me stress and made me wonder, just for a second, "Is it worth it?"

Educators must be willing to press through students' tears, sarcasm, or anger and provide an atmosphere of supportive confrontation in which students are both respected and challenged to think beyond their own experiences. While validating students' opinions and feelings, teachers must also be willing to explore multicultural materials that invite critical analysis. Such curriculum must be coupled with pedagogy that asks challenging questions and that does not back down from difficult or uncomfortable class discussions.

Supporting Teachers

If teachers are to provide an environment that addresses racial power and privilege, they too will need support. Schools have not traditionally challenged oppressive systems; instead, they have more often functioned to preserve the racial status quo (Bonilla-Silva and Embrick 2008). Educational systems that offer unequal scholastic experiences to students, whether through failing schools populated by students of color on state or district levels or through academic tracking within schools, are at risk of reproducing social and racial inequity. Teachers will need both school-wide and system-wide support in order to recognize that they are part of this system and to pursue an antiracist agenda.

Almost a year after I finished my fieldwork at EA I received an e-mail from Lisa, the teacher who had spoken of her discomfort over "racially charged" situations in her classroom. Lisa asked me for suggestions on readings that might help white teachers learn how to more effectively teach African American students. Of course, I was happy to provide suggestions for Lisa and the other teachers and glad that she viewed me as a resource. However, I was struck by the fact that while Lisa and most of her colleagues had been teaching for many years, they sensed their own lack of preparedness in educating black students. Further, the kind of resources Lisa sought were not readily available from her school administration. Over the years state departments of education have undergone many changes in their teacher preparation programs, and those changes have not always included training for preservice teachers in critical multicultural education. State teacher preparation guidelines tend to focus on "family and community," a heading that incorporates a broad range of subjects and may or may not address racism and other societal inequities. Thus, it is entirely possible for preservice teachers in EA's home state to graduate from teacher education programs never having discussed racism or engaged in critical pedagogy of any kind. Joann, in fact, who had graduated from a well-respected state university, told me that except for a course in feminist literary criticism, she had not studied critical pedagogy in her preservice courses. Christine E. Sleeter (2001) reports that when teacher education programs do include multicultural coursework, preservice teachers continue to think of addressing diversity as a matter of learning new teaching techniques or multicultural content curriculum and do not understand the need to address the underlying structural causes and effects of racism. Her meta-analysis concludes that the lasting benefit of college-level multicultural coursework is unclear, but that teacher education programs that include "community-based immersion experiences" (102) show the most promising results. Avner Segall and James Garrett (2013) note that while white pre- and in-service teachers possess sufficient content knowledge about racism, they avoid admitting this knowledge in order to escape the reflection and attitudinal changes that such knowledge might require. The authors, themselves teacher educators, conclude that engaging college students in discussions of racism is not enough. Students need help in unpacking how their unexamined "narrative frames" (i.e., deep-seated social and political beliefs influenced by neoliberal ideals of meritocracy and individualism) inform their constructions of "other" and their own meaning-making processes (288). Therefore, while I commend the teachers at EA for their desire to learn how to address race in their classrooms, I also must note that these teachers were inadequately prepared for this task in their teacher education programs, and that much-needed professional training in this area is not available through their school.

The Need for Self-Reflection

The wording of Lisa's request also showed that she and other white teachers saw the gulf between themselves and their African American students as a matter of cultural competency and not as the result of centuries of white dominance. Consequently, they did not appreciate the importance of self-reflection in exploring the function of race in the classroom; rather, they were looking for how-to, quick-fix methodology to "reach" their African American students. Instead of quick-fix pedagogical tips, white teachers need support and training to help them engage in the critical self-reflection that examines their own positions of privilege in a highly racialized system (Naidoo 1992). As a white teacher, what assumptions do I make about my students? Do my expectations of students' achievement vary based on their racial background, gender, socioeconomic status, or other factors? Do I affirm the cultural and language styles of all students, or do I view those of the white students as "normal" and all others as exotic or as culturally and intellectually inferior? Do I engage all students in critical thinking? Are my assessment practices fair, or are they biased toward those of the dominant group? Perhaps most importantly, do I recognize the multiple ways in which my whiteness worked for me when I was a student, and the invisible but powerful way it works for me still? Or do I believe that my effort alone is responsible for my career success? If I am honest, I will admit that even after years of asking myself these questions, the meritocratic thinking of neoliberal whiteness discourse can easily creep into my pedagogy and relationships with students. How easy it is, for example, to write off students as not being "ready" for the rigors of college course work without considering and finding ways to counteract the racist educational system that left them unprepared. How easy it is to place full responsibility for lack of academic progress on students without examining more carefully how my colleagues and I might have worked harder to keep these students engaged. Without careful and consistent self-reflection, white teachers like me may unknowingly reproduce a racist societal structure in our classrooms and schools through our academic policies and practices (Bonilla-Silva and Embrick 2008).

A strong impediment to self-reflection is the view that teachers are experts whose job is to impart knowledge while students are novices waiting to be filled with information. When applied to exploring race in the classroom, this "banking" model of education (Freire 1970, 72) ignores the process of identity construction and assumes that learning information about racism is all that is needed for students to incorporate antiracist attitudes. As we saw, EA students had learned about racism in previous school years, but that knowledge did little to help white students understand the perspectives of their friends of color. Beverley Naidoo (1992) reassures us that "when students see their teacher involved in the same process of questioning and self-scrutiny," those students are better prepared to "combine affective with cognitive knowledge" (146). Teachers who engage in self-reflection with their students model a process of growth that blends cognitive understandings and affective dispositions in the construction of racial identity.

From the beginning of my fieldwork, Joann had been committed to ideals of social justice, and over the months I witnessed a progression in her understandings and feelings about race. I heard her go from claiming colorblindness in our initial meeting ("I don't notice my students' racial backgrounds") to telling a group of students early in my research, "There are no races. There is only one human race," to a frustrated admission to me privately, "I still hate the idea of races. We should all be just the human race. But I know now that race is a social construct and that racism is real and we have to deal with it." Joann and I had many private conversations in which her questions to me showed that she was working hard to construct a white racial identity that was thoroughly antiracist. Sustained, reflective conversations about race helped Joann to deepen her perspective on a topic about which she cared very much.

However, through the stories she told students about her experiences with race, Joann was always careful to present the persona of one who had "arrived" at antiracism. She did not reflect on her process of "figuring it out" with students. Likewise, I said nothing about my own process of racial identity formation as a white person but instead came across as an "expert" whose goal it was to convert students to my way of thinking. Joann exacerbated this image of me by commenting to her classes from time to time how "lucky" they were to have a college professor to participate in their literature units. Although I was uncomfortable with the image of myself that Joann projected to the students, I said nothing to correct her. By not modeling ourselves as whites in the process of coming to terms with our whiteness, Joann and I denied white students the role models that may have been helpful to them, and denied students of color the opportunity to understand white racial identity formation through our eyes. While our sincere desire was to help white students incorporate antiracist attitudes into their racial identity, we stopped short of personalizing white dominance in our conversations with students. Lisa Mazzei's (2011) work on desiring silence may partly explain our behavior; while we continually challenged students through course curriculum from which we were emotionally detached, our desire to maintain a personal distance from students and to uphold our roles as authority figures—roles entwined with our whiteness—kept us from exploring our own positions of dominance and privilege with students and limited how far we were willing to go in exposing our personal struggles with racism to them.

Teachers who do engage in critical self-reflection model the process of constructing racial identities that incorporate antiracism. While recognizing that teachers will approach multicultural literature in their curriculum from differing levels of racial awareness, Naidoo (1992) encourages white teachers, especially, to "acknowledge themselves as co-learners in the process of reperception" (148). Teachers can model their process of racial identity construction by talking with their students about their experiences as racialized people and by openly describing how their own thinking and feelings regarding race continue to develop and be refined throughout life.

Looking at Teachers' Silence

While I have spent much time analyzing students' silences, Mazzei (2007) also insists that researchers probe their own silences as meaningful parts of the speech continuum. Of course, as this study has shown, there were many times that Joann and I responded to students' comments and probed them for clarification. Albeit far less frequently, there were also those times that we were silent and allowed students' responses to remain unexamined. For example, why were Joann and I silent when Lyssa remarked, "I'm light-skinned, so that's not an issue," directly after we had viewed the Davis (2007) video, *A Girl Like Me?* Why didn't one of us ask, "What do you mean by that, Lyssa? What isn't an issue for you, and why? How does your statement position you in relation to the girls in the video, or the other girls in this class?"

Some of our silences were surely due to the fast pace of class discussions, but at times during this project my silence stemmed from uncertainty regarding my role as participant observer in the classroom. How much instruction should I offer students about racism, and how much should I allow them to lead the discussion? How much did I "really want to hear their voices," as Joann had told students, and how should I handle it when those voices led to the perpetuation of racist discourse? McIntyre (1997) explains the anxiety she felt in her research with white preservice teachers. She describes how she felt "paralyzed with inadequacy" (32) after she had failed to challenge the racist assumptions of her participants. Striking the right balance between encouraging students' honest expression of ideas and challenging racist discourse was difficult. If Joann and I had problematized our silence through self-reflection, as Mazzei (2007) suggests, we may have become cognizant of how silence reflected the uncertainty and complacency embedded within our own racial identities. Such awareness may have helped prepare us to address the silences of students in the days to come.

Getting Past Anxiety

Anxieties about accusations of racism may also hinder Joann and other white teachers from engaging in honest conversations about race that include insights they have gained through self-reflection. If it is difficult for teachers to talk about race through use of curricular materials, addressing the issue on a personal basis will be more difficult still. Joann was one of the only teachers at EA who persisted in her efforts to include race in her curriculum, despite student and administrative resistance. The one other teacher who was known to talk about race with her students *was* accused of racism by a student and fired later in the school year for undisclosed reasons. Teachers like Joann would very likely fear professional ramifications were students to perceive their statements or questions as admissions of racist thoughts or feelings, making such conversations highly risky business. Teachers need assurances that discussion about race, including reflections regarding their own racial identity development, will not leave them vulnerable to possible accusations of racism.

Concluding Thoughts: Looking Beyond the Friendships

When I began this project, my goal was to ascertain how students constructed ideas about race as they read and discussed multicultural literature in the classroom. I wondered if studying works meant to depict racial oppression would help students to broaden their understandings of how race continues to work as a stratifying agent in society. I found that engagement with multicultural literature did create opportunity for students to think, feel, and talk about race. However, during my time at EA I also observed students working through racial identity through language, cultural group membership, and physical appearance—aspects of their daily lives that had little to do with the texts they studied. It was clear to me that proximity to students of racial backgrounds other than their own made race visible to students every day (Lewis 2006; Perry 2002).

Most importantly, the mixed-race setting at EA gave students the opportunity to form consistent cross-racial friendships. These friendships engendered a feeling of group unity and safety that made for a peaceful and productive educational experience for students. Students at EA did not experience the overt tension that a student at a mixed-race school described to Perry (2002): "You're kind of playing a game to get through the day and not offend anybody. Everything is so, you know, tense, usually, in a way. . . . Like, walking down the hall, the people that will usually tease me or yell at me or call me a bitch or will stand in my way and not let me down the hallway, tend not to be white" (158). I observed none of this type of behavior at EA, where teachers were able to focus on the business of teaching and not on maintaining order among warring factions of students.

The existence of cross-racial friendships, however, is not enough to ensure racial equity on a system-wide level, nor are those friendships a guarantee that students' racial identities will incorporate antiracist understandings. Indeed, at this friendly, racially harmonious school, I found that racial tensions thrived covertly. Both white and African American students felt that their points of view were not acknowledged and harbored feelings of marginalization, frustration, and anger over perceived racial favoring. White students and teachers feared accusations of racism that, for teachers, threatened their sense of job security. Further, a racially harmonious atmosphere is not necessarily an indication that all students are receiving the same quality of educational experience; at EA, students of color were kept from important curricular content because of racially biased judgments on the part of school administrators. Cross-racial friendships also influenced class discussion dynamics by encouraging silence for some students while giving others the confidence to deny the salience of racism and of their own position of racial privilege.

As wonderful and important as cross-racial friendships are, the notion that they alone are indicators of open, honest race relations and antiracist ideals in students and teachers is problematic. Unless schools like EA examine how race functions in their environment, they run the risk of reproducing racial inequity. Without a doubt, teachers and administrators should foster an environment where cross-racial friendships flourish. At the same time, we must not neglect the deeper analysis of how race functions to create and maintain power structures in the midst of, and perhaps because of, those friendships.

Appendix A

Studying Race in the Suburbs:
More on Methods

Excellence Academy, the site of this research, is a charter school: that is, it is publicly funded but privately operated. Charter schools are not controlled by the public school districts in which they are housed but, because they are public schools, must be nonsectarian and may not charge tuition. According to the state department of education website, individuals or groups wanting to start a "brick and mortar" charter school (i.e., a traditional school, not a cyber school) must apply for a "charter" from their host school district showing that their school offers an education that is innovative and distinctive from that offered by the district-run public schools. Amid a fairly hostile reception from the teachers and administrators of the Woodlark Area School District, EA opened its doors in 2000 as a corporately run charter school but has since cut ties with its corporate founder. EA defines itself as an award-winning college-prep school whose mission is to prepare a diverse group of students for school and life success.

Area Demographics

Although EA is a majority-white school, it is more racially diverse than Woodlark, its host district, and Brookside, the closest neighboring school district. Thirty-one percent of students at EA live in Woodlark, 9 percent are from the Brookside School District, and 36 percent travel daily from the Carltonville Area School District. The remaining 24 percent of EA's students come from eighteen different school districts in the surrounding area. The community of Carltonville is larger and more racially diverse than Woodlark, and many of the students in Joann's classes would have attended Carltonville High School (located approximately twelve miles away) had they not been enrolled at EA. Table 1 shows the racial and economic demographics of EA compared with that of the Woodlark and Brookside school districts and with Carltonville High School. Since the Carltonville School District is so much larger than Woodlark and Brookside districts, comprising eleven schools in neighborhoods with vastly differing economic and racial demographics, I felt it more pertinent to compare EA with the only high school in the district and not with the entire district.

Information about the Excellence Academy Charter School came from the school's Registrar, in an e-mail dated May 2012. Information about the Woodlark Local and Brookside School Districts, and about Carltonville High School came from the National Center for Education Statistics, http://nces.ed.gov, 2012–2013 school year. Please note that some racial demographic statistics equal less than 100% due to rounding.

Table 1: Comparison of EA with Neighboring Districts

	Excellence Academy Charter School	Woodlark Local School District	Brookside School District	Carltonville High School
Total Students	987	3,431	7,859	1,739
White	60%	80.6%	84.2%	32.3%
African American / Black	20%	7.2%	4.3%	44.9%
Multiracial	9%	1%	2.9%	1.2%
Asian / Pacific Islander	5%	3.6%	5.3%	1.7%
Hispanic	5%	7.3%	3%	19.6%
American Indian / Alaskan	0%	0%	0%	0.1%
Free or Reduced Lunch	26%	20%	8%	53%

Class Demographics

Table 2 provides the racial demographics of Joann's literature classes. Although the student body at EA was racially diverse, with the exception of a few individuals, the faculty, administration, and staff were almost exclusively white.

Table 2: Racial Demographic of Literature Classes

Class	Total # Students	White (%)	African American (%)	Asian (%)	Hispanic (%)	Biracial (%)
10th Grade On-Level	15	60	40	0	0	0
10th Grade Honors	26	65	15	15	4	0
11th Grade On-Level	26	42	54	0	0	4
11th Grade Honors	23	65	30	4	0	0

All percentages are rounded to the nearest hundredth.

The Texts

Interestingly, the only difference in choice of texts for the on-level and honors classes of either grade level was the substitution of *The Catcher in the Rye* for *The Bluest Eye* in the eleventh grade on-level class, an administrative decision dripping with race and social class bias that I analyze in chapter 1.

Table 3: Texts Studied by EA Students

Class	Literature
10th Grade On-Level and Honors	*Macbeth*, by William Shakespeare *The Woman Warrior*, by Maxine Hong Kingston *A Long Way Gone*, by Ishmael Beah *Night*, by Elie Wiesel *The Kite Runner*, Khaled Hosseini
11th Grade On-Level	*The Scarlet Letter*, by Nathaniel Hawthorne Harlem Renaissance Unit *The Great Gatsby*, by F. Scott Fitzgerald *The Crucible*, by Arthur Miller *The Catcher in the Rye*, by J. D. Salinger
11th Grade Honors	*The Scarlet Letter*, by Nathaniel Hawthorne Harlem Renaissance Unit *The Great Gatsby*, by F. Scott Fitzgerald *The Crucible*, by Arthur Miller *The Bluest Eye*, by Toni Morrison

My Role as Researcher

My role of participant observer allowed me to actively engage with students at some times and to quietly observe them at others. During my times of quiet observation, I had access to my computer, which allowed me to document student conversations and class discussions either as they were happening or shortly after. Segments of field notes that I analyze in this book were recorded in this manner. Often I was more active, contributing to small and large-group class discussions, sometimes at Joann's request but often at my own discretion based on my interest in the conversations that were taking place. Again, I was usually able to document these discussions in writing directly after they took place, and if I couldn't remember exactly what students had said, Joann, whose memory was better than mine, would remind me. Therefore, although my field notes are not direct transcriptions of digital recordings, I believe they are accurate representations of the discussions that transpired in the classroom.

Along with taking daily field notes, I wrote memos to ponder what I was seeing and hearing, and I conducted twenty-six interviews: twenty with students, five with teachers, and one with a school administrator. My interviews took on the unstructured quality of ethnographic interviews that, Bucholtz (2011) notes, are meant to be "relatively informal interactions oriented to the cultural concerns and norms of the interviewee rather than the interviewer" (37). I found that interviews were an indispensable way to follow up with students and teachers about discussions or situations I had witnessed in class or that Joann had told me about. I recorded interviews and transcribed them shortly thereafter. Segments from interviews included in this study are direct transcriptions in which I did not edit grammar, although I did use ellipses to indicate brief omissions that were needed to maintain clarity and flow.

In addition, I had access to students' written school assignments and to information published on the school website. Students' written assignments were important to my study because they sometimes told a deeper story than that which I would have seen or heard, had I depended on observation or interviews alone. Finally, on a few occasions I wrote and presented lessons to Joann's classes that used a combined childist / critical race approach to the texts. This approach and my reflections on these lessons are described in appendix B. An example of a lesson I taught on *The Bluest Eye* is included in appendix C.

When my fieldwork reached its conclusion, I coded field notes, memos, interview transcripts, e-mails, and students' written work to see what themes regarding race and racism emerged. Many critical race / whiteness researchers have found rhetorical patterns or discourses that whites, especially, engage in when faced with the issue of race, including silence, incoherence, and colorblind and reverse racism arguments (Bonilla-Silva 2006; Haviland 2008; Marx 2006; McIntyre 1997; Pollock 2004). I looked for these patterns of discourse among whites while taking note of other patterns that emerged from my data. I also noted the responses of students of color in Joann's classes and analyzed cross-race and within-race interactions among students and student–teacher interactions. Thus, my study combines existing theory with grounded theory (that which I formulate from my own data) (Maxwell 2005).

My participation in Joann's classes varied according to the needs of the students and the assigned texts. Many of the texts studied, especially by the eleventh grade, did not fall under the general rubric of multicultural literature or particularly lend themselves to discussions of racial oppression (despite some white students' insistence that race was "all we ever talk about"). However, from the outset I believed that every day I spent at EA was valuable in two ways. First, I knew it would take time to establish my presence in the school and to get to know the students. I intentionally did not conduct any student interviews until the latter part of my fieldwork, partly because it took that long to collect parental consent forms but mostly because I felt I needed time to build relationships and trust with students. Second, the many hours I spent quietly observing students when they *weren't* discussing multicultural texts were crucial in helping me discover how students performed race informally through cultural styles that incorporated physical appearance, language, speech, and other outward behaviors. I wanted to understand not only what students thought about race as they read multicultural texts but also how they acted out their racial identities on a daily basis.

I admit that there were a few occasions when I suspected that the performance of race was being executed for my benefit. For example, one African American eleventh grader who told me to call her "Rihanna" would sometimes break out in snippets of a rap and then smile mischievously in my direction. However, for the most part students adjusted to my presence quite quickly and ignored me as they did the many other adults that came and went in their classroom. While most of my time was spent in the classroom, I also observed students and teachers at lunch, a school pep rally, an African Dance Troupe presentation (meant as a celebration of Black History Month), and on a field trip to the U.S. Holocaust Memorial Museum in Washington, D.C. In this way I gained insight about students' relationships with one another and with their teachers as I witnessed many informal interactions and associations in a variety of settings (Maxwell 2005).

A dilemma I faced at the beginning of my fieldwork at EA involved how to explain my presence to students. Since I knew from talking to Joann that students and teachers did not often discuss race outwardly, I worried that some would shut down immediately if I told them from the outset that I was there to study their ideas about race. I decided to take the approach used by Beverley Naidoo (1992), and on my first day I simply told the students that I was interested in their responses to the literature they would be reading in class. Then, as time progressed and we began to read literature that dealt more specifically with racial oppression, I explained to students that I was especially interested in their views on race and racism. This allowed for a warming up period that, I hope, encouraged students to speak openly and honestly during small- and large-group class discussions.

As should be expected, my relationship with students changed over time. Once the initial adjustment period passed, students routinely caught my eye and smirked during Joann's mini-lectures, complained to me if they didn't understand an assignment she had given, and confessed when they didn't do the readings (a common occurrence even among the honors students). At times my biggest struggle as a classroom participant was to keep a straight face during some very funny student antics, but while I did not want to appear as an authority figure to the students, I also needed to be careful not to undermine Joann's authority. So, although blending in with the students was not an option, by rejecting a position of teacher-like authority I do believe I was able to achieve, if not least-adult (Mandell 1988), perhaps lesser-adult status. John, a white tenth grader, tested this status by addressing me by my first name, a cultural taboo at EA and most other K–12 schools. "Hi, Marianne!" he would shout whenever he entered the room or saw me in the hallway. "Hi, John!" I would respond cheerfully, as the other students laughed and shook their heads. Of course, I'm not implying that students routinely included me in private conversations about important personal issues. Although there were a few times that students, at Joann's prompting, allowed my presence as they shared personal struggles with her, there were many more times when students' conversations about someone getting arrested, someone in trouble with the dean, or someone fighting with parents ended abruptly when I came near. Still, although the invisible wall that separates students from teachers was certainly present in my classroom interactions with students, I believe students allowed me a few windows through which I could witness their daily exchanges with one another.

Appendix B

The Childist/Critical Race
Approach

My background as educator and my familiarity with childhood studies and critical race scholarship made me wonder how students might respond to a combined childist / critical race literary critique of the multicultural texts they were assigned. I saw lessons constructed using this approach as a way to blend the theoretical frameworks of childhood studies and critical race theory through my project. In keeping with John Wall's (2010) concept of *childism*, a childist approach to literary criticism considers historical and philosophical constructions of children and childhood, adult–child relationships and boundary crossing, and an exploration of childhood as a site of marginalization. Such an approach complements and intersects with the application of other areas of literary criticism that explore the concerns of marginalized or oppressed groups. Therefore, a combined childist / critical race critique might explore the adult/child role reversals that take place between the white child characters and adult characters of color in a text, compare and contrast age and racial/ethnic oppression experienced by characters, or consider historical and philosophical views of childhood and compare them to how people of color are treated or viewed in the text. My goal in presenting these lessons was to discover if students who might not relate to racially oppressed characters would, because of their youth, relate to characters who were either marginalized because of age and race, or who, through racism, were denied adult status. With this in mind, on a few occasions I wrote and presented lessons to Joann's classes that used this combined childist / critical race approach to the texts.

Joann was more than willing to give me opportunity to teach my lessons, usually asking me to fill in for her when she needed to be out of the room to proctor standardized tests or attend meetings. Although I constructed lesson materials for tenth grade classes reading *The Woman Warrior*, *A Long Way Gone*, and *The Kite Runner*, space prohibits me from analyzing student responses to these works. Therefore, I refer now to my experience in sharing the curricular materials I developed during *The Bluest Eye* unit for 11 Honors.

Due to shortened class periods because of standardized testing, my lesson actually took place over three class sessions at the very beginning of *The Bluest Eye* unit. Students seemed most interested in the early parts of the lesson that asked them to reflect on their views about childhood and whether or not children are treated as full citizens in our society. We then discussed ways in which the child characters of *The Bluest Eye* were marginalized during the opening pages of the novel, and we ended by comparing children with other groups who have been marginalized throughout history, such as women and African Americans.

Students were polite and engaged during my lessons. However, while my childist / critical race lesson construction was unique in that other curricular aids do not typically take this approach, students' responses to my lessons were not particularly indicative of their deeply felt ideas and opinions about race; rather, these feelings were more strongly expressed during the use of other curricular materials that I have described in chapters 2, 3, and 4. Although I believe my lessons may have increased students' understandings of the events of the story and of the motivations of the characters, in the end they represented just one more adult-led activity through which students were expected to answer questions that would be counted toward their class participation grade. I found that these honors students, concerned with keeping their grades high, were quite adept at the question/answer participation structure that is prevalent in our educational system. Unfortunately, students' answers to my discussion questions revealed little about their understanding of racism as a current issue or of their own racial identities. They simply answered questions about a story that took place many decades ago and had little to do with their present context.

Students' responses during my lessons did show that they were interested in thinking about childhood differently than they had done before, and in viewing it as a possible site of marginalization, but later on in the unit both James and Anthony mentioned "the childist thing" and "kids' rights," respectively, as topics that students were tired of talking about. I felt that my lessons did little to "draw on students' hearts and give those feelings of human connection combined status with the head" (Naidoo 1992, 144). Of course, I'm not implying that students should be required to respond emotionally to curriculum, or that teachers should purposely provoke an emotional response from students in order to judge the effectiveness of their lessons. However, in the case of 11 Honors, students' later responses to *The Bluest Eye* showed that they did harbor deep and complicated feelings about race, but it wasn't until Joann presented supplementary curricular materials that intentionally pointed out how racism exists today, specifically the *Race: The Power of an Illusion* (2003) video and the McIntosh (2005) essay, that students allowed those emotions to surface through passionate class discussions. Perhaps the effectiveness of these curricular tools in promoting discussion above the lessons I constructed points, again, to the need to offer students materials that explore racism in their present context.

Appendix C

Childist/Critical Race
Lesson for 11 Honors

The Bluest Eye

Objectives:

> Students will describe three historical/philosophical constructions of childhood.
>
> Students will analyze various depictions of childhood in the opening sections of text.
>
> Students will compare childhood with other sites of marginalization, such as race or gender.

Motivation:

In groups of four, describe your favorite childhood memory. Why is this memory important to you? Then name your favorite TV show or movie in which children are the main characters. Why is it your favorite?

Development:

We all have favorites that we can remember from childhood. Memories of our own lives or images from popular culture often stay with us because they represent something to us. You may remember some things from childhood and not others because they represent something important about childhood.

Brainstorm the following questions in groups: What is childhood? What adjectives pop into your mind when you think about children? Add your responses to the board.

Talking and thinking about childhood is nothing new. People's ideas about childhood have shifted a great deal over the centuries. A scholar named John Wall (2010) talks about three basic views of childhood that have existed since ancient times.

1. *Top-down* (Plato, Augustine, Calvin)—children are like animals: they are unreasonable and need training. The job of adults is to control and train children. Example—Bible verse, "Spare the rod and spoil the child." This was reflected in the Puritan belief that children are sinful.
2. *Bottom-up* (Rousseau)—children demonstrate humanity's goodness; they are innocent and pure. The job of adults is to protect children and keep them innocent as long as possible. Advertisements capitalize on this view of childhood all the time, as in the antismoking public service announcement from the Child Health Foundation (figure 1).
3. *Developmental* (Aristotle, Aquinas, Locke)—children are "blank slates." They will become whatever their environment makes them. The job of adults is to teach them and help them develop in healthy ways. This is reflected in the famous poem, "Children Learn What They Live," by Dorothy Law Nolte.

Discussion Questions:

Which of these views of childhood were evident in *The Crucible*?

What are some other views of childhood that we can add to this list?

Another way that some scholars think about childhood is as a time of marginalization. Suppose you were an attorney representing not one person but childhood. How might you argue that children are not full citizens? What specific aspects of childhood would you point out in a court of law?

Part of my research is to introduce a specific way of critiquing texts to you and to get your opinions about this critique. I call this a combined

Children of parents who smoke, get to heaven earlier.

FIGURE 1: Child Health Foundation Public Service Announcement
Reproduced by permission of Child Health Foundation, Dr. von Hauner Children's Hospital, University of Munich, Germany. http://www.kindergesundheit.de.

childist / critical race critique—I look at how both race and childhood are depicted in the text and how both of these work together to impact characters in the text.

> Question: In what ways might we compare children with other groups who have been marginalized throughout history, such as women, African Americans, etc. (can you think of others)?

Further Discussion Questions about *The Bluest Eye*:

1. What does Claudia tell us about her childhood in the first few pages of the novel? What views of childhood are depicted here?
2. In what ways are Claudia and her sister marginalized within their family?
3. We know that Claudia is looking back at her childhood as an adult as she relates the incidents that take place at the beginning of the novel. Is that important, and if so, why?
4. How did race and age intersect to affect the way characters were treated in the story?

Notes

Introduction

1 All names of participants, schools, and places in this study are pseudonyms.

2 For more information on contemporary racial disparity, see The Sentencing Project, "Racial Disparity in the Criminal Justice System" (2000), http://www.sentencingproject.org/template/page.cfm?id=122; E. Ann Carson and William J. Sabol, "Prisoners in 2011," *Bureau of Justice Statistics Bulletin* (December 2012), http http://bjs.gov/content/pub/pdf/p11.pdf; and United States Census Bureau, "Income, Expenditures, Poverty & Wealth," *The 2012 Statistical Abstract*, http://www.census.gov/compendia/statab/cats/income_expenditures_poverty_wealth/poverty.html.

3 Some scholars have critiqued Helms's work as pseudo-science (Rowe 2006). Regardless of this critique, the approach developed by Helms and others has had a major impact on thinking about racial identity development. Stephen M. Quintana (2007) notes that while not all assumptions of developmental racial identity models are supported by longitudinal data, these models remain an important tool in exploring identity development with youth.

4 See appendix A for complete information on demographics and the qualitative methods this study involved.

1 Boundaries among Friends

1 The only attempt to interrupt students' racial clustering came not from teachers or administration but from the student council, who sponsored a "mix-it-up" lunch period that all students and teachers were required to attend. After having their hands stamped when they entered the cafeteria, students were told to sit at the table with the picture that matched their stamp. This random stamping should have resulted in racially mixed tables but did not; the black/white divide continued. Black and white students seated at the same tables tended to split themselves down the center with each group choosing opposite ends.

2 Anger among Friends

1 One might argue that these performers, well intentioned as they were, serve as an example of white appropriation of someone else's culture and history for their own gain.

3 Discourse among Friends

1 My friendship with Violet first developed through the following circumstance: Joann had left the room for a moment, leaving me in charge while students (supposedly) worked quietly at their desks. Within a minute of her departure, several paper airplanes began flying through the air, and one, launched by Violet, hit me lightly in the eye. Violet was mortified and apologized profusely, but I joked about it, holding my eye dramatically as if the plane had done serious damage. When Joann returned we acted as if nothing had happened, and she never found out what had taken place in her absence. For a while the airplane incident became a running joke between Violet and me, and perhaps my silence about the event earned me a small amount of "cred" in her eyes.

2 Retrieved from the Poetry Foundation website, http://www.poetryfoundation.org/poem/175884.

3 "Historical retrojection" is a term used often by biblical scholars to describe interpretation of biblical events based on societal needs or beliefs that come into being long after the events have taken place. Jeffrey Siker (2007), for example, explores "how modern biblical scholarship has contributed to the historicizing and retrojection of a racialized Jesus" (26).

4 Resistance among Friends

1 Gillborn (2009) makes an important distinction between "whiteness" as a discourse and white people as a socially constructed identity group. White people may or may not espouse the discourse of whiteness, just as heterosexual people may or may not be homophobic.

2 Space prohibits me from exploring another argument some students employed to complain about several of the books they'd been assigned. Ron, James, and others devalued fiction, failing to see it as "truth" when compared to nonfiction.

3 Students' writing is reproduced exactly, with no grammatical or spelling corrections.

References

Aboud, Frances E., Morton J. Mendelson, and Kelly T. Purdy. 2003. "Cross-Race Peer Relations and Friendship Quality." *International Journal of Behavioral Development* 27, no. 2: 165–173.

Abrams, Lyndon, and Jerry Trusty. 2004. "African Americans' Racial Identity and Socially Desirable Responding: An Empirical Model." *Journal of Counseling & Development* 82: 365–374.

Anacker, Katrin B. 2010. "Still Paying the Race Tax? Analyzing Property Values in Homogeneous and Mixed-Race Suburbs." *Journal of Urban Affairs* 32, no. 1: 55–77.

Angelou, Maya. 1969. *I Know Why the Caged Bird Sings.* New York: Random House.

Anzaldúa, Gloria. 1999. *Borderlands: The New Mestizo.* 3rd ed. San Francisco: Aunt Lute Books.

Apfelbaum, Evan P., Samuel R. Sommers, and Michael I. Norton. 2008. "Seeing Race and Seeming Racist? Evaluating Strategic Colorblind Social Interaction." *Journal of Personality and Social Psychology* 95, no. 4: 918–932.

Baldwin, Bridgette. 2009. "Colorblind Diversity: The Changing Significance of 'Race' in the Post-*Bakke* Era." *Albany Law Review* 72, no. 4: 863–890.

Balfanz, Robert, and Nettie Legters. 2004. *Locating the Dropout Crisis.* Report prepared for the Center for Research on the Education of Students Placed at Risk, John Hopkins University.

Banks, Lynne Reid. 1980. *The Indian in the Cupboard.* New York: Doubleday.

Bass, Loretta E. 2010. "Childhood in Sociology and Society: The US Perspective." *Current Sociology* 58, no. 29: 335–350.

Beach, Richard, Amanda Haertling Thein, and Daryl Parks. 2008. *High School Students' Competing Social Worlds.* New York: Routledge.

Beah, Ishmael. 2007. *A Long Way Gone.* New York: Sarah Crichton Books.

Bell, Derrick. 1987. *And We Are Not Saved: The Elusive Quest for Racial Justice.* New York: Basic Books.

———. 1992. *Faces at the Bottom of the Well: The Permanence of Racism.* New York: Basic Books.

———. 2000. "Property Rights in Whiteness: Their Legal Legacy, Their Economic Costs." In *Critical Race Theory: The Cutting Edge*, ed. Richard Delgado, and Jean Stefancic, 71–79. Philadelphia: Temple University Press.

———. 2009. "*Brown v. Board of Education* and the Interest Convergence Dilemma." In *Foundations of Critical Race Theory in Education*, ed. Edward Taylor, David Gillborn, and Gloria Ladson-Billings, 73–84. New York: Routledge.

Bishop, John H., Matthew Bishop, Michael Bishop, Lara Gelbwasser, Shanna Green, Erica Peterson, Anna Rubinsztaj, and Andrew Zuckerman. 2004. "Why We Harass Nerds and Freaks: A Formal Theory of Student Culture and Norms." *Journal of School Health* 74, no. 7: 235–251.

Bonilla-Silva, Eduardo. 2006. *Racism without Racists: Color-Blind Racism and the Persistence of Racial Inequality in the United States*. Lanham, MD: Rowman & Littlefield.

Bonilla-Silva, Eduardo, and David G. Embrick. 2008. "Recognizing the Likelihood of Reproducing Racism." In *Everyday Antiracism*, ed. Mica Pollock, 334–336. New York: New Press.

Botelho, Maria J., and Masha Kabakow Rudman. 2009. *Critical Multicultural Analysis of Children's Literature*. New York: Routledge.

Brooks, Wanda. 2008. "Reading Representations of Themselves: Urban Youth Use Culture and African American Textual Features to Develop Literary Understandings." *Reading Research Quarterly* 41, no. 3: 372–392.

Bucholtz, Mary. 2011. *White Kids: Language, Race, and Styles of Youth Identity*. Cambridge: Cambridge University Press.

Burton, Linda M., Eduardo Bonilla-Silva, Victor Ray, Rose Buckelew, and Elizabeth Hordge Freeman. 2010. "Critical Race Theories, Colorism, and the Decade's Research on Families of Color." *Journal of Marriage and Family* 72: 440–459.

Bush, Melanie. 2004. *Breaking the Code of Good Intentions: Everyday Forms of Whiteness*. Lanham, MD: Rowman & Littlefield.

Carter, Prudence L. 2005. *Keepin' It Real: School Success beyond Black and White*. New York: Oxford University Press.

———. 2012. *Stubborn Roots: Race, Culture, and Inequality in U.S. and South African Schools*. New York: Oxford University Press.

Carter, Robert T., Janet E. Helms, and Heather L. Juby. 2004. "The Relationship between Racism and Racial Identity for White Americans: A Profile Analysis." *Journal of Multicultural Counseling and Development* 32: 2–17.

Cerezo, Alison, Benedict T. McWhirter, Diana Peña, Marina Valdez, and Cristina Bustos. 2013. "Giving Voice: Utilizing Critical Race Theory to Facilitate Consciousness of Racial Identity of Latina/o College Students." *Journal for Social Action in Counseling and Psychology* 5, no. 3: 1–24.

Chadwick, Jocelyn. 2008. "Teaching Racially Sensitive Literature." In *Everyday Antiracism*, ed. Mica Pollock, 195–198. New York: New Press.

Chalmers, Virginia. 1997. "White Out: Multicultural Performances in a Progressive School." In *Off White: Readings on Race, Power, and Society*, ed. Michelle Fine, Lois Weis, Linda C. Powell, and L. Mun Wong, 66–78. New York: Routledge.

Chin, Elizabeth. 1999. "Ethnically Correct Dolls: Toying with the Race Industry." *American Anthropologist* 101, no. 2: 305–321.

Choi, Jung-ah. 2008. "Unlearning Colorblind Ideologies in Education Class." *Educational Foundations* 22, no. 3–4: 53–71.

Christerson, Brad, Korie L. Edwards, and Richard Flory. 2010. *Growing Up in America: The Power of Race in the Lives of Teens*. Stanford, CA: Stanford University Press.

Cochran-Smith, Marilyn. 2004. "Blind Vision: Unlearning Racism." In *Facing Racism in Education Teacher Education*, ed. Sonya Anderson, Polly F. Attwood, and Lionel C. Howard, 277–309. Cambridge, MA: Harvard Education Publishing Group.

Davis, Kiri, dir. 2007. *A Girl Like Me*. Sixth Annual Media that Matters Film Festival. YouTube, May 4. http://www.youtube.com/watch?v=YWyI77Yh1Gg.

DeCuir, Jessica T., and Adrienne D. Dixson. 2004. "So When It Comes Out, They Aren't That Surprised That It Is There: Using Critical Race Theory as a Tool of Analysis of Race and Racism in Education." *Educational Researcher* 33, no. 5: 26–31.

de Freitas, Elizabeth, and Alexander McAuley. 2008. "Teaching for Diversity by Troubling Whiteness: Strategies for Classrooms in Isolated White Communities." *Race Ethnicity and Education* 11, no. 4: 429–442.

Delgado, Richard, and Jean Stefancic. 2000. *Critical Race Theory: The Cutting Edge*. Philadelphia: Temple University Press.

Delpit, Lisa D. 2004. "The Silenced Dialogue: Power and Pedagogy in Educating Other People's Children." In *Facing Racism in Education*, ed. Sonya Anderson, Polly F. Attwood, and Lionel C. Howard, 123–143. Cambridge, MA: Harvard Education Publishing Group.

DiAngelo, Robin. 2006. "My Class Didn't Trump My Race: Using Oppression to Face Privilege." *Multicultural Perspectives* 8, no. 1: 52–56.

Dickens, Angelia. 1996. "Revisiting *Brown v. Board of Education*: How Tracking Has Resegregated America's Public Schools." *Columbia Journal of Law and Social Problems* 469: 469–506.

Dixson, Adrienne D., and Celia K. Rousseau. 2005. "And We Are Still Not Saved: Critical Race Theory in Education Ten Years Later." *Race Ethnicity and Education* 8, no. 1: 7–27.

Du Bois, W.E.B. (1903) 2005. *The Souls of Black Folk*. Reprint, New York: Simon and Schuster.

Durden, Tonia R., and Diane M. Truscott. 2013. "Critical Reflectivity and the Development of New Culturally Relevant Teachers." *Multicultural Perspectives* 15, no. 2: 73–80.

Emond, Ruth. 2009. "Ethnographic Research Methods with Children and Young People." In *Researching Children's Experiences*, ed. Sheila Greene and Diane Hogan, 123–139. Los Angeles: Sage.

Erickson, Frederick. 1987. "Transformation and School Success: The Politics and Culture of Educational Achievement." *Anthropology & Education Quarterly* 18, no. 4: 335–356.

Fine, Michelle. 1997. "Witnessing Whiteness." In *Off White: Readings on Race, Power, and Society*, ed. Michelle Fine, Lois Weis, Linda C. Powell, and L. Mun Wong, 57–65. New York: Routledge.

Flynn, Jill E. 2012. "Critical Pedaogy with the Oppressed and the Oppressors: Middle School Students Discuss Racism and White Privilege." *Middle Grades Research Journal* 7, no. 2: 95–110.

Fordham, Signithia, and John Ogbu. 1986. "Black Students' School Success: Coping with the Burden of 'Acting White.'" *Urban Review* 18: 176–206.

Forsey, Martin. 2004. "'He's Not a Spy; He's One of Us': Ethnographic Positioning in a Middle-Class Setting." In *Anthropologists in the Field*, ed. Lynne Hume, and Jane Mulcock, 59–70. New York: Columbia University Press.

Frankenberg, Ruth. 1993. *White Women, Race Matters: The Social Construction of Whiteness*. Minneapolis: University of Minnesota Press.

Freire, Paulo. 1970. *Pedagogy of the Oppressed*. New York: Continuum International.

Frontline. 1985. "A Class Divided." First broadcast March 26. Directed by William Peters and written by William Peters and Charlie Cobb.

Gallagher, Charles A. 2003. "Color-Blind Privilege: The Social and Political Functions of Erasing the Color Line in Post-Race America." *RGC Journal Special Edition on Privilege* 10, no. 4: 575–588.

Gates, Henry Louis, Jr. 1988. *The Signifying Monkey: A Theory of African American Literary Criticism.* New York: Oxford University Press.

Gillborn, David. 2009. "Education Policy as an Act of White Supremacy: Whiteness, Critical Race Theory, and Education Reform." In *Foundations of Critical Race Theory in Education*, ed. Edward Taylor, David Gillborn, and Gloria Ladson-Billings, 51–69. New York: Routledge.

Giroux, Henry A. 2008. *Against the Terror of Neoliberalism.* Boulder, CO: Paradigm Publishers.

Greene, Stuart, and Dawn Abt-Perkins. 2003. *Making Race Visible: Literacy Research for Cultural Understanding.* New York: Teachers College Press.

Haney López, Ian F. 2000. "The Social Construction of Race." In *Critical Race Theory: The Cutting Edge*, ed. Richard Delgado, and Jean Stefancic, 163–175. Philadelphia: Temple University Press.

———. 2011. "Is the 'Post' in Post-Racial the 'Blind' in Colorblind?" *Cardozo Law Review* 32, 3: 807–831.

Harris, Cheryl I. 1993. "Whiteness as Property." *Harvard Law Review* 106, no. 8: 1710–1791.

Harris, Frank, III, and Laura E. Struve. 2009. "Gents, Jerks, and Jocks: What Male Students Learn about Masculinity in College." *About Campus* 14, no. 3: 2–9.

Haviland, Victoria S. 2008. "'Things Get Glossed Over': Rearticulating the Silencing Power of Whiteness in Education." *Journal of Teacher Education* 59, no. 1: 40–54.

Hawthorne, Nathaniel. (1850) 1984. *The Scarlet Letter.* Reprint, Pleasantville, NY: Reader's Digest Association.

Hays, Diana, Catherine Y. Chang, and Pamela Havice. 2008. "White Racial Identity Statuses as Predictors of White Privilege." *Journal of Humanistic Counseling, Education & Development* 47, no. 1: 234–246.

Helms, Janet E. 1990. *Black and White Racial Identity.* Westport, CT: Praeger.

———. 2007. "Some Better Practices for Measuring Racial and Ethnic Identity Constructs." *Journal of Counseling Psychology* 54, no. 3: 235–246.

Hernandez, Donald J., Nancy A. Denton, and Victoria L. Blanchard. 2011. "Children in the United States of America: A Statistical Portrait by Race-Ethnicity, Immigrant Origins, and Language." *Annals of the American Academy of Political and Social Science* 633: 102–127.

Hollingworth, Liz. 2009. "Complicated Conversations: Exploring Race and Ideology in an Elementary Classroom." *Urban Education* 44, no. 1: 30–57.

Hughes, Langston. 1994a. "Harlem (2)." In *The Collected Poems of Langston Hughes*, ed. Arnold Rampersad and David Roessel, 426. New York: Random House.

———. 1994b. "I, Too." In *The Collected Poems of Langston Hughes*, ed. Arnold Rampersad and David Roessel, 46. New York: Random House.

Hume, Lynne, and Jane Mulcock. 2004. *Anthropologists in the Field.* New York: Columbia University Press.

Hutchinson, George B. 1992. "Langston Hughes and the 'Other' Whitman." In *The Continuing Presence of Walt Whitman*, ed. Robert K. Martin, 16–27. Iowa City: University of Iowa Press.

James, Allison. 2007. "Giving Voice to Children's Voices: Practices and Problems, Pitfalls and Potentials." *American Anthropologist* 109, no. 2: 261–272.

Jenks, Chris. 1996. *Childhood*. Abingdon: Routledge.

Kao, Grace, and Kara Joyner. 2004. "Do Race and Ethnicity Matter among Friends? Activities among Interracial, Interethnic, and Intraethnic Adolescent Friends." *Sociological Quarterly* 45, no. 3: 557–573.

Katz, Judith H. 1978. *White Awareness: Handbook for Anti-Racism Training*. Norman: University of Oklahoma Press.

Kendall, Lori. 2011. "'White and Nerdy': Computers, Race, and the Nerd Stereotype." *Journal of Popular Culture* 44, no. 3: 505–524.

Killen, Melanie, Megan Clark Kelly, Cameron Richardson, David Crystal, and Martin Ruck. 2010. "European American Children's and Adolescents' Evaluations of Interracial Exclusion." *Group Processes & Intergroup Relations* 13, no. 3: 283–300.

Kromidas, Maria. 2012. "Affiliation or Appropriation? Crossing and the Politics of Race among Children in New York City." *Childhood* 19, no. 3: 317–331.

Kubitschek, Warren, and Maureen Hallinan. 1998. "Tracking and Students' Friendships." *Social Psychology Quarterly* 61, no. 1: 1–15.

Kumasi, Kafi D. 2011. "Critical Race Theory and Education: Mapping a Legacy of Activism and Scholarship." In *Beyond Critique: Exploring Critical Social Theories and Education*, ed. Bradley A. U. Levinson, 196–219. Boulder, CO: Paradigm Publishers.

Ladson-Billings, Gloria. 2009. *The Dreamkeepers: Successful Teachers of African American Children*. 2nd ed. San Francisco: Wiley.

Ladson-Billings, Gloria, and William F. Tate IV. 1995. "Toward a Critical Race Theory of Education." *Teachers College Record* 97, no. 1: 47–68.

Lashbrook, Jeffrey T. 2000. "Fitting In: Exploring the Emotional Dimension of Adolescent Peer Pressure." *Adolescence* 35, no. 140: 747–757.

Law, Sylvia A. 1999. "White Privilege and Affirmative Action." *Akron Law Review* 32, no. 3: 603–626.

Lee, Harper. 1960. *To Kill a Mockingbird*. New York: Warner Books.

Leonardo, Zeus. 2002. "The Souls of White Folk: Critical Pedagogy, Whiteness Studies, and Globalization Discourse." *Race Ethnicity and Education* 5, no. 1: 29–50.

Lester, Neal A. 2000. "Nappy Edges and Goldy Locks: African American Daughters and the Politics of Hair." *The Lion and the Unicorn* 24, no. 2: 201–224.

Lewis, Amanda. 2006. *Race in the Schoolyard*. New Brunswick, NJ: Rutgers University Press.

Lewis, R. L'Heureux. 2010. "Speaking the Unspeakable: Youth Discourses on Racial Importance in School." In *Sociological Studies of Children and Youth*. Vol. 13, *Children and Youth Speak for Themselves*, ed. Heather Beth Johnson, 401–421. Bingley, UK: Emerald Group Publishing.

Lewis-Charp, Heather. 2003. "Breaking the Silence: White Students' Perspectives on Race in Multiracial Schools." *Phi Delta Kappan* 85, no. 4 (December): 279–285.

Logan, John R. 2011. *Separate and Unequal: The Neighborhood Gap for Blacks, Hispanics, and Asians in Metropolitan American*. Report prepared for the US2010 Project, Brown University.

Lueck, Kerstin, and Hayley Steffen. 2011. "White Kids: Identity Construction, Critical Mass, and Symbolic Exclusion in High School Cliques and Other Groups." *Berkeley Review of Education* 2, no. 1: 46–67.

Lukes, Steven. 2005. *Power: A Radical View*. 2nd ed. London: Palgrave Macmillan.

Luther, Kristin. 2009. "Celebration and Separation: A Troublesome Approach to Multicultural Education." *Multicultural Perspectives* 11, no. 4: 211–216.

MacLeod, Jay. 2009. *Ain't No Makin' It: Aspirations and Attainment in a Low-Income Neighborhood*. Boulder, CO: Westview Press.

Majors, Richard. 2001. "Cool Pose: Black Masculinity and Sports." In *The Masculinities Reader*, ed. Stephen M. Whitehead and Frank J. Barrett, 209–217. Cambridge: Polity Press.

Mandell, Nancy. 1988. "The Least-Adult Role in Studying Children." *Journal of Contemporary Ethnography* 16, no. 4: 433–467.

Marx, Sherry. 2006. *Revealing the Invisible: Confronting Passive Racism in Teacher Education*. New York: Routledge.

Matrenec, Ravi Hansra. 2011. "The Struggle for Identity for African American Adolescent Males in a Predominantly White, Affluent School." *Journal of Poverty* 15, no. 2: 226–240.

Maxwell, Joseph A. 2005. *Qualitative Research Design: An Interactive Approach*. Thousand Oaks, CA: Sage Publications Inc.

May, Stephen, and Christine E. Sleeter. 2010. "Introduction." In *Critical Multiculturalism: Theory and Praxis*, ed. Stephen May and Christine E. Sleeter. New York: Routledge.

Mazzei, Lisa A. 2007. "Toward a Problematic of Silence in Action Research." *Educational Action Research* 15, no. 4: 631–642.

———. 2008. "Silence Speaks: Whiteness Revealed in the Absence of Voice." *Teaching and Teacher Education* 24: 1125–1136.

———. 2011. "Desiring Silence: Gender, Race, and Pedagogy in Education." *British Educational Research Journal* 37, no. 4: 657–669.

McCarthy, Cameron, and Greg Dimitriadis. 2005. "Governmentality and the Sociology of Education: Media, Educational Policy, and the Politics of Resentment." In *Race, Identity, and Representation in Education*, ed. Cameron McCarthy, Warren Crichlow, Greg Dimitriadis, and Nadine Dolby, 321–335. New York: Routledge.

McIntosh, Peggy. 2005. "White Privilege: Unpacking the Invisible Knapsack." In *White Privilege: Essential Readings on the Other Side of Racism*, ed. Paula. S. Rothenberg, 109–114. New York: Worth Publishers.

McIntyre, Alice. 1997. *Making Meaning of Whiteness: Exploring Racial Identity with White Teachers*. Albany: State University of New York Press.

Meyer, Stephen. 2000. *As Long as They Don't Move Next Door: Segregation and Racial Conflict in American Neighborhoods*. Lanham, MD: Rowman & Littlefield.

Mills, Carmen, and Trevor Gale. 2007. "Researching Social Inequalities in Education: Towards a Bourdieuian Methodology." *International Journal of Qualitative Studies in Education* 20, no. 4: 433–447.

Modica, Marianne. 2012. "Constructions of Race among Religiously Conservative College Students." *Multicultural Perspectives* 14, no. 1: 38–43.

Morrison, Toni. 1970. *The Bluest Eye*. New York: Alfred A. Knopf.

———. 1993. *Playing in the Dark*. New York: Random House.

Munniksma, Anke, and Jaana Juvonen. 2012. "Cross-Ethnic Friendships and Sense of Social-Emotional Safety in a Multiethnic Middle School: An Exploratory Study." *Merrill-Palmer Quarterly* 58, no. 4: 489–506.

Naidoo, Beverley. 1992. *Through Whose Eyes? Exploring Racism: Reader, Text, and Context*. London: Trentham Books.

Nakkula, Michael J., and Eric Toshalis. 2008. *Understanding Youth: Adolescent Development for Educators*. Cambridge, MA: Harvard Education Press.

Nieto, Sonia. 2005. "School Reform and Student Learning: A Multicultural Perspective." In *Multicultural Education: Issues and Perspectives*, ed. James A. Banks and Cherry A. McGee Banks, 401–420. Hoboken, NJ: John Wiley & Sons.

Oakes, Jeannie. 2005. *Keeping Track*. 2nd ed. New Haven, CT: Yale University Press.

Ochoa, Gilda L., and Daniela Pineda. 2008. "Deconstructing Power, Privilege, and Silence in the Classroom." *Radical History Review* 102: 45–62.

Ogbu, John U. 2004. "Collective Identity and the Burden of 'Acting White' in Black History, Community, and Education." *Urban Review* 36, no. 1: 1–35.

Page-Gould, Elizabeth, Rodolfo Mendozo-Denton, and Linda R. Tropp. 2008. "With a Little Help from My Cross-Group Friend: Reducing Anxiety in Intergroup Contexts through Cross-Group Friendship." *Journal of Personality and Social Psychology* 95, no. 5: 1080–1094.

Pascoe, C. J. 2007. *Dude, You're a Fag: Masculinity and Sexuality in High School*. Berkeley: University of California Press.

Penn, Helen. 2008, *Understanding Early Childhood: Issues and Controversies*. New York: Open University Press.

Perry, Imani. 2011. *More Beautiful and More Terrible: The Embrace and Transcendence of Racial Inequality in the United States*. New York: New York University Press.

Perry, Pamela. 2002. *Shades of White: White Kids and Racial Identities in High School*. Durham, NC: Duke University Press.

———. 2008. "Creating Safe Spaces in Predominantly White Classrooms." In *Everyday Antiracism*, ed. Mica Pollock, 226–229. New York: New Press.

Pettigrew, Alice. 2012. "Confronting the Limits of Antiracist and Multicultural Education: White Students' Reflections on Identity and Difference in a Multiethnic Secondary School." *Sociological Research Online* 17, no. 3: 1–11.

Pollock, Mica. 2004. *Colormute: Race Talk Dilemmas in an American School*. Princeton, NJ: Princeton University Press.

Pratt, Mary Louise. 1998. "Arts of the Contact Zone." In *Negotiating Academic Literacies: Teaching and Learning across Languages and Cultures*, ed. Vivian Zamel and Ruth Spack, 171–186. Mahwah, NJ: Lawrence Erlbaum.

Quillian, Lincoln, and Mary E. Campbell. 2003. "Beyond Black and White: The Present and Future of Multiracial Friendship Segregation." *American Sociological Review* 68, no. 4: 540–566.

Quintana, Stephen M. 2007. "Racial and Ethnic Identity: Developmental Perspectives and Research." *Journal of Counseling Psychology* 54, no. 3: 259–270.

Race: The Power of an Illusion. "The House We Live In." 2003. Written, produced, and directed by Llewellyn M. Smith. San Francisco: California Newsreel. DVD.

Rentzch, Katrin, Astrid Schütz, and Michela Schröder-Abé. 2011. "Being Labeled *Nerd*: Factors That Influence the Social Acceptance of High-Achieving Students." *Journal of Experimental Education* 79: 143–168.

Roediger, David R. 1992. *The Wages of Whiteness: Race and the Making of the American Working Class*. New York: Verso.

———. 1994. *Towards the Abolition of Whiteness*. New York: Verso.

Rosenbloom, Susan Rakosi. 2010. "Dis-Identity in a Multiracial Urban High School." In *Sociological Studies of Children and Youth*. Vol. 13, *Children and Youth Speak for Themselves*, ed. Heather Beth Johnson, 3–31. Bingley, UK: Emerald Group Publishing.

Rowe, Wayne. 2006. "White Racial Identity: Science, Faith, and Pseudoscience." *Journal of Multicultural Counseling and Development* 34: 235–243.

Rude, Jesse, and Daniel Herda. 2010. "Best Friends Forever? Race and the Stability of Adolescent Friendships." *Social Forces* 89, no. 2: 585–607.

Said, Edward W. 1979. *Orientalism*. New York: Vintage Books.

Salter, Phia, and Glenn Adams. 2013. "Toward a Critical Race Psychology." *Social and Personality Psychology Compass* 7, no. 11: 781–793.

Samson, Frank L. 2013. "Altering Public University Admission Standards to Preserve White Group Position in the United States: Results from a Laboratory Experiment." *Comparative Education Review* 57, no. 3: 369–396.

Saul, Wendy, and Kendra Wallace. 2002. "Centering the Margins: White Preservice Teachers' Responses to *Roll of Thunder*." *Teaching Education* 13, no. 1: 41–53.

Schultz, Katherine. 2008. "Interrogating Students' Silences." In *Everyday Antiracism*, ed. Mica Pollock, 217–221. New York: New Press.

———. 2009. *Rethinking Classroom Participation: Listening to Silent Voices*. New York: Teachers College Press.

Segall, Avner, and James Garrett. 2013. "White Teachers Talking Race." *Teaching Education* 24: 265–291.

Seitles, Marc. 1998. "The Perpetuation of Residential Racial Segregation in America: Historical Discrimination, Modern Forms of Exclusion, and Inclusionary Remedies." *Journal of Land Use & Environmental Law* 14 (1). http://archive.law.fsu.edu/journals/landuse/Vol141/seit.htm.

Shankar, Shalini. 2008. *Desiland: Teen Culture, Class, and Success in Silicon Valley*. Durham, NC: Duke University Press.

Siker, Jeffrey S. 2007. "Historicizing a Racialized Jesus: Case Studies in the 'Black Christ,' the 'Mestizo Christ,' and White Critique." *Biblical Interpretation* 15: 26–53.

Silvestri, Timothy J., and Tina Q. Richardson. 2001. "White Racial Identity Statuses and NEO Personality Constructs: An Exploratory Analysis." *Journal of Counseling & Development* 79 (Winter): 68–76.

Sleeter, Christine. 2001. "Preparing Teachers for Culturally Diverse Schools: Research and the Overwhelming Presence of Whiteness." *Journal of Teacher Education* 52, no. 2: 94–106.

———. 2005. "How White Teachers Construct Race." In *Race, Identity, and Representation in Education*, ed. Cameron McCarthy, Warren Crichlow, Greg Dimitriadis, and Nadine Dolby, 243–256. New York: Routledge.

Solorzano, Daniel G., and Tara J. Yosso. 2009. "Critical Race Methodology: Counter-Storytelling as an Analytical Framework for Educational Research." In *Foundations of Critical Race Theory in Education*, ed. Edward Taylor, David Gillborn, and Gloria Ladson-Billings, 131–147. New York: Routledge.

Song, Miri. 2001. "Comparing Minorities' Ethnic Options: Do Asian Americans Possess 'More' Ethnic Options than African Americans?" *Ethnicities* 1, no. 1: 57–82.

Staiger, Annegret. 2005. "Recreating Blackness-as-Failure through Educational Reform? A Case Study of a California Partnership Academy." *Equity & Excellence in Education* 38: 35–48.

Stoughton, Edy Hammong, and Connie Sivertson. 2005. "Communicating across Cultures: Discursive Challenges and Racial Identity Formation in Narratives of Middle School Students." *Race Ethnicity and Education* 8, no. 3: 277–295.

Sue, Derald Wing, Christina M. Capodilupo, Gina C. Torino, Jennifer M. Bucceri, Aisha M. B. Holder, Kevin L. Nadal, and Marta Esquilin. 2007. "Racial Microaggressions in Everyday Life." *American Psychologist* 62, no. 4: 271–286.

Tarca, Katherine. 2005. "Colorblind in Control: The Risks of Resisting Difference amid Demographic Change." *Educational Studies* 30, no. 2: 99–120.

Tatum, Beverly Daniel. 1997. *"Why Are All the Black Kids Sitting Together in the Cafeteria?" and Other Conversations about Race.* New York: Basic Books.

Tavares, Carlos Daniel. 2011. "Why Can't We Be Friends: The Role of Religious Congregation-Based Social Contact for Close Interracial Adolescent Friendships." *Review of Religious Research* 52, no. 4: 439–453.

Taylor, Edward. 2009. "The Foundations of Critical Race Theory in Education: An Introduction." In *Foundations of Critical Race Theory in Education*, ed. Edward Taylor, David Gillborn, and Gloria Ladson-Billings, 1–16. New York: Routledge.

Taylor, Mildred. 1976. *Roll of Thunder, Hear My Cry.* New York: Puffin Books.

Thomas, Mary E. 2011. *Multicultural Girlhood: Racism, Sexuality, and the Conflicted Spaces of American Education.* Philadelphia: Temple University Press.

Thomas, Pierre, and Jason Ryan. 2009. "Stinging Remarks on Race from Attorney General." *ABC News, February 18.* http://abcnews.go.com/TheLaw/story?id=6905255.

Tisdall, E. Kay M., and Samantha Punch. 2012. "Not So 'New'? Looking Critically at Childhood Studies." *Children's Geographies* 10, no. 3: 249–264.

Trainor, Jennifer Seibel. 2008. *Rethinking Racism: Emotion, Persuasion, and Literacy Education in an All-White High School.* Carbondale: Southern Illinois University Press.

Twain, Mark. (1884) 1996. *Adventures of Huckleberry Finn.* Reprint, New York: Random House.

Tyson, Karolyn. 2011. *Integration Interrupted: Tracking, Black Students, and Acting White after Brown.* New York: Oxford University Press.

Van Ausdale, Debra, and Joe R. Feagin. 2001. *The First R: How Children Learn Race and Racism.* Lanham, MD: Rowman & Littlefield.

Wall, John. 2010. *Ethics in Light of Childhood.* Washington, DC: Georgetown University Press.

Waters, Mary C. 2001. *Black Identities: West Indian Immigrant Dreams and American Realities.* Cambridge, MA: Harvard University Press.

Welton, Anjalé D. 2013. "Even More Racially Isolated Than Before: Problematizing the Vision for 'Diversity' in a Racially Mixed High School." *Teacher College Record* 115 (November): 1–42.

Wiesel, Elie. 1960. *Night.* New York: Hill and Wang.

Winkler, Erin. 2012. *Learning Race, Learning Place: Shaping Racial Identities and Ideas in African American Childhoods.* New Brunswick, NJ: Rutgers University Press.

Whitman, Walt. 2007. "I Hear America Singing." In *Leaves of Grass: The Original 1855 Edition*, 17. Mineola, NY: Dover Publications.

Wong, Paul, Chienping Faith Lai, Richard Nagasawa, and Tieming Lin. 1998. "Asian Americans as a Model Minority: Self-Perceptions and Perceptions by Other Racial Groups." *Sociological Perspectives* 41, no. 1: 95–108.

Worrell, Frank C., William E. Cross Jr., and Beverly J. Vandiver. 2001. "Nigrescence Theory: Current Status and Challenges for the Future." *Journal of Multicultural Counseling and Development* 29: 201–213.

Youdell, Deborah. 2004. "Identity Traps; or, How Black Students Fail: The Interactions between Biographical, Sub-cultural, and Learner Identities." In *The RoutledgeFalmer Reader in Multicultural Education*, ed. Gloria Ladson-Billings and David Gillborn, 84–102. London: RoutledgeFalmer.

Index

About the Author

MARIANNE MODICA is an associate professor of education at University of Valley Forge.

CPSIA information can be obtained at www.ICGtesting.com
Printed in the USA
LVOW08s0354051115

461206LV00003B/161/P